The Last Journey

A Guide to Palliative Care and

The Dying Process

By

Omomaro Okekaro, PhD

Copyright by Omomaro Okekaro, 2024
ISBN: 979-8-9897804-2-6

Printed in the USA, 2024

Table of Contents

Introduction

The Last Journey: A Guide to Palliative Care and the Dying Process is a comprehensive guide to understanding the final stages of life. The book provides an in-depth look at the dying process, including physical and emotional symptoms, and the role of palliative care. The guide is designed to provide comfort and support to those who are facing the end-of-life journey, whether it is for themselves or for a loved one. The book is written in a clear and accessible manner, with the aim of demystifying the process and helping readers feel more confident and prepared for what lies ahead. Whether you are a healthcare professional, a caregiver, or someone simply seeking to better understand the end of life, *The Last Journey* is an essential resource that will provide valuable insight, guidance, and comfort during this challenging time.

The statement, "life is about what is important to you, how you want to live, and how you want to die" is a powerful reminder of the importance of taking control of our own lives. It highlights that life is not just about surviving, but about living in a way that is fulfilling, meaningful, and true to our values and beliefs. By understanding what is truly important to us and what we want to achieve in our lives, we can make choices and take actions that align with our goals and bring us closer to living the life we want. Additionally, the statement also highlights the importance of considering how we want to die and what kind of care we want at the end of our lives. It is important to have open and honest conversations about death and dying and to make informed decisions about our care and well-being as we approach the end of our lives.

This statement also highlights the importance of living a meaningful life and the impact that one's actions and choices can have on their legacy and the memories they leave behind. It emphasizes the need to prioritize what is truly important to us and to make choices that align with our values and goals. By doing so, we can ensure that we live a life filled with purpose and that our memory lives on in a positive way. This perspective can be a source of comfort and motivation as we navigate the ups and downs of life and face the inevitability of death.

Overview of End-of-Life Journey

In the end-of-life journey, individuals are faced with physical, emotional, and spiritual challenges as they approach the final stages of life. This period can be a time of reflection and preparation, and it is important for individuals to be informed and supported as they navigate this transition. *The Last Journey: A Guide to Palliative Care and the Dying Process* aims to provide individuals and their loved ones with information, support, and resources to help make this time more manageable. This guide covers the physical and emotional changes that may occur during the dying process, the role of palliative care, and the importance of self-care, family support, and professional resources. The guide also explores the impact of cultural and religious beliefs on the end-of-life journey and provides guidance for families with children and adolescents who are grieving. This book is an essential resource for anyone facing the end of life journey and is seeking support, comfort, and understanding.

Chapter 1
Understanding Palliative Care

Palliative care is a holistic approach to care that addresses the physical, emotional, spiritual, and social needs of individuals and families during the dying process. It focuses on relieving symptoms, improving quality of life, and supporting both the patient and their loved ones through the physical, emotional, and spiritual challenges of serious illness. It aims to provide comfort, support, and dignity to adults failing to thrive and those who are facing a life-limiting illness. The goal of palliative care is to help individuals and families navigate the planes of transition with greater ease and grace, and to provide them with the support they need to cope with the dying process.

Palliative care can be provided alongside curative treatments and is intended to complement, not replace other medical care. It is a team-based approach that involves a variety of healthcare professionals, including doctors, nurses, social workers, chaplains, and others. The team works together to address physical, emotional, and spiritual needs, and to support patients and their families in making informed decisions about their care.

One of the key features of palliative care is that it is patient-centered and focuses on the individual's unique needs and preferences. It is not limited to end-of-life care, but can be provided at any stage of a serious illness, from diagnosis through recovery or bereavement.

Palliative care is appropriate for individuals with a variety of serious illnesses, such as cancer, heart failure, chronic obstructive pulmonary disease (COPD), kidney disease, and others. It can be provided at any stage of an illness, from diagnosis to end of life, and can be delivered alongside other treatments, such as chemotherapy or radiation therapy.

It is important to note that palliative care is not the same as hospice care, although hospice care is a type of palliative care. Hospice care is specifically for individuals who are expected to have six months or less to live and focuses on comfort and quality of life rather than cure. Palliative care, on the other hand, can be provided at any stage of an illness and can be combined with other treatments.

Palliative care is a crucial aspect of the end-of-life journey, providing support and comfort to individuals and their families during a difficult and challenging time. By addressing the physical, emotional, social, and spiritual needs of the patient and their family, palliative care can help improve the quality of life and provide a sense of peace and comfort. Understanding these processes can help ensure that individuals receive the appropriate care, and that their loved ones can offer meaningful support. Key components of palliative care include:

Pain and symptom management

Ensuring that the patient is as comfortable as possible by addressing any pain or discomfort they may be experiencing.

Emotional and psychological support

Providing a safe space for the patient and their family to express their feelings, fears, and concerns, as well as offering counseling or spiritual support as needed.

Care coordination

Collaborating with other healthcare professionals to ensure the patient's needs are met and that care is consistent and well-managed.

Advance care planning

Helping the patient and their family make informed decisions about their care preferences and goals, including any necessary legal or financial arrangements.

Benefits of Palliative Care

The benefits of palliative care are numerous and can help to ease the burden of serious illness for both the patient and their loved ones. Some of the key benefits of include:

Alleviating symptoms

Palliative care can help to relieve the physical, emotional, and spiritual symptoms that often arise from serious illness. This can include pain management, symptom control, and management of other symptoms such as fatigue, shortness of breath, and anxiety.

Improving quality of life

Palliative care is focused on improving quality of life for the patient and their family. This can involve addressing the patient's physical, emotional, and spiritual needs, as well as providing support for the family as they navigate the end-of-life journey.

Coordinating care

Palliative care can help to coordinate the care provided by different healthcare professionals, ensuring that the patient receives the right care at the right time. This can reduce confusion and ensure that the patient's needs are met in a timely and effective manner.

Supporting the family

Palliative care can provide support for the family as they navigate the end-of-life journey. This can include emotional support, practical support, and education on how to care for the patient.

Reducing costs

Palliative care can help to reduce healthcare costs by reducing the need for unnecessary treatments and hospitalizations, and by providing more cost-effective care for the patient.

A Holistic Approach to Care

Holistic care is an approach to healthcare that considers the whole person, including their physical, emotional, spiritual, and social well-being. It is a comprehensive approach that seeks to address all aspects of a person's life, not just their medical condition. The goal of holistic care is to help people live as fully and comfortably as possible, even as they face serious illness or the end of life.

A holistic approach to care recognizes that each person is unique, and that their individual needs and experiences must be taken into account when providing care. This can include everything from physical symptoms and treatments to emotional support and spiritual guidance. By considering all of these factors, healthcare providers can create a care plan that addresses the whole person and helps them to feel supported and comforted as they navigate a challenging time.

In the context of palliative care, a holistic approach is especially important. By taking a holistic approach, healthcare providers can ensure that their patients receive the best possible care, and that their experience of illness or the end-of-life care is better managed both pain and symptom free.

Managing Pain and Symptoms

Pain and symptoms can be physical, emotional, spiritual, or mental and can significantly affect the quality of life for individuals and their loved ones. Pain management is an essential part of palliative care, and it aims to relieve discomfort, prevent suffering, and improve quality of life.

There are various methods for managing pain, including medications, such as opioids, and non-medication treatments, like massage and acupuncture. In addition to managing pain, palliative care also focuses on managing other symptoms, such as nausea, vomiting, and constipation, which can be caused by diseases or treatments.

Palliative care teams work closely with individuals and their families to understand their specific needs and preferences, and to develop a comprehensive care plan that addresses all aspects of their care, including pain and symptom management. By providing comprehensive and individualized care, palliative care helps individuals maintain their dignity, comfort, and quality of life during their end-of-life journey.

With the support of a palliative care team, individuals and their families can focus on the meaningful moments and memories they create together, rather than the physical discomfort and suffering associated with their illness.

Coping with Emotional and Spiritual Distress

Coping with emotional and spiritual distress during the end-of-life journey is a critical aspect of palliative care. It is important to understand that the end-of-life journey is not just about managing physical symptoms, but also about addressing the emotional and spiritual needs of the individual and their loved ones.

Emotional and spiritual distress can manifest in many different ways, including feelings of fear, anxiety, depression, anger, and guilt. The palliative care team will work with the individual and their loved ones to help manage these feelings and provide support during this challenging time. This may include individual counseling sessions, group therapy, or spiritual support from a chaplain or other spiritual leader.

In addition to addressing emotional and spiritual distress, palliative care can also help individuals and their families understand and cope with the realities of death and the end-of-life journey. This may include having open and honest conversations about the individual's wishes, end-of-life goals, and any other concerns or fears they may have.

By addressing both physical and emotional-spiritual needs, palliative care can play an important role in improving the quality of life for individuals during this challenging time. To analyze the experience of coping with emotional and spiritual distress, consider the following aspects:

Recognizing the signs

Emotional and spiritual distress can manifest as feelings of depression, anxiety, anger, guilt, hopelessness, or a sense of isolation. Recognizing these signs and acknowledging the individual's distress is the first step in providing appropriate support and guidance.

Providing emotional support

Healthcare professionals and loved ones can offer emotional support by listening empathetically, validating the individual's feelings, and offering comforting words or insights. Encouraging open communication and providing a safe, nonjudgmental environment can help individuals process their emotions and feel understood.

Addressing spiritual concerns

For many individuals, emotional distress may be closely tied to spiritual concerns or a crisis of faith. Healthcare professionals and loved ones should approach these issues with sensitivity, respecting the individual's beliefs and values while offering spiritual support and guidance as appropriate. This may involve facilitating discussions about existential questions, connecting the individual with a spiritual leader or counselor, or offering resources such as prayer, meditation, or spiritual texts.

Encouraging therapeutic interventions

Various therapeutic interventions can help individuals cope with emotional and spiritual distress, including counseling, support groups, art therapy, music therapy, or mindfulness practices. These resources can provide individuals with a structured and supportive setting to explore their emotions, address their spiritual concerns, and develop coping strategies.

Fostering resilience and personal growth

Coping with emotional and spiritual distress can offer individuals an opportunity for personal growth and the development of emotional resilience. By facing their challenges and seeking support, individuals may cultivate a deeper sense of self-awareness, compassion, and inner strength.

Understanding the experience of coping with emotional and spiritual distress during the end-of-life journey or grieving process can help healthcare professionals and loved ones provide the necessary support and guidance. By offering emotional and spiritual support, encouraging therapeutic interventions, and fostering resilience and personal growth, we can create a nurturing environment for individuals to navigate their challenges and find healing and solace in their circumstances.

Building Relationships with Hospice Caregivers

Building relationships with hospice caregivers is an important part of the palliative care experience. Hospice care is designed to provide comfort and support to individuals who are facing a life-limiting illness, and this care is delivered by a team of healthcare professionals who are trained in addressing the physical, emotional, and spiritual needs of patients and their families.

Having a strong relationship with hospice caregivers can help individuals and families feel more comfortable and supported during this difficult time. Hospice caregivers are there to listen, offer guidance and support, and provide care that is tailored to the individual's needs. They can help to address symptoms, provide emotional support, and offer spiritual guidance, as needed.

It is important for individuals and families to build trust and open communication with hospice caregivers. This can be done by asking questions, sharing concerns, and providing feedback. It is also important to be honest and open about the individual's needs and preferences, as this will help the hospice team to provide the best possible care.

Ultimately, building relationships with hospice caregivers can help individuals and families navigate the dying process with greater comfort and peace of mind. By working together, individuals, families, and hospice teams can ensure that the end of life journey is one of dignity, comfort, and support.

Building relationships with hospice caregivers is an essential aspect of ensuring a positive end-of-life experience for individuals and their families. Hospice caregivers play a crucial role in providing emotional, physical, and spiritual support during the final stages of life, and fostering strong relationships with them can lead to improved communication, trust, and overall care. To analyze the experience of building relationships with hospice caregivers, consider the following aspects:

Open communication

Establishing open lines of communication with hospice caregivers is key to building a strong and trusting relationship. By sharing information about the individual's needs, preferences, and concerns, family members and caregivers can collaborate more effectively to provide the best possible care.

Mutual respect

Building relationships with hospice caregivers requires mutual respect and understanding. Recognizing the expertise and compassion that caregivers bring to their work can foster a sense of trust and facilitate a more harmonious caregiving environment.

Involvement in care

Encouraging family members to participate in the individual's care, alongside hospice caregivers, can strengthen relationships and create a sense of shared responsibility. This involvement can range from assisting with personal care tasks to participating in care planning meetings and decision-making processes.

Emotional support

Hospice caregivers often provide emotional support to both individuals and their families, helping them navigate the complex emotions that accompany the end-of-life journey. Developing a strong emotional connection with caregivers can lead to more meaningful and effective support during this challenging time.

Cultural and spiritual considerations

Respecting and acknowledging the individual's cultural and spiritual beliefs is crucial in building relationships with hospice caregivers. By understanding and accommodating these beliefs, caregivers can provide more personalized and compassionate care.

Ongoing feedback and collaboration

Regularly providing feedback and maintaining open dialogue with hospice caregivers can help ensure that the individual's needs are being met and any concerns are addressed promptly. This collaboration can also foster a sense of teamwork and shared purpose in providing the best possible care.

Building relationships with hospice caregivers is a vital aspect of ensuring a positive end-of-life experience for individuals and their families. By fostering open communication, mutual respect, and ongoing collaboration, healthcare professionals, family members, and hospice caregivers can work together to provide the highest level of compassionate and personalized care during this challenging time.

The Dying Process and Palliative Care

The dying process and palliative care are important aspects of end-of-life care, as they focus on providing comfort, relief from pain, and emotional support for patients and their families during the final stages of life. Understanding these processes can help ensure that individuals receive the appropriate care, and that their loved ones can offer meaningful support.

Chapter 2
Understanding the Dying Process

The dying process refers to the physical and emotional changes that occur as an individual approaches the end of life. It is a unique experience for each person and can be unpredictable, but it is important to understand the common changes that may occur. Physical symptoms, such as changes in breathing, alterations in temperature, and fatigue, are often experienced by individuals in the dying process. Emotional and psychological changes, such as confusion, decreased engagement with the environment, and decreased communication, may also occur.

This process is a natural progression that occurs as the body begins to shut down. By understanding the dying process and the principles of palliative care, healthcare providers, patients, and families can work together to create a compassionate and supportive environment during the final stages of life. This approach allows the patient to maintain their dignity and quality of life, while also providing comfort and solace for their loved ones.

This process can vary in duration and symptoms but typically involves several stages: the pre-active stage, the active stage, and the transition stage, of each will be discussed in more depth in the following chapter.

In order to provide proper care and support to a loved one who is dying, it is important to understand the dying process and what to expect. This can help alleviate fear and reduce stress for both the individual and their caregivers. The dying process can also be a time for meaningful reflection, spiritual growth, and emotional healing. By approaching the end of life with open communication, compassion, and understanding, it is possible to create a peaceful and supportive environment for all involved.

In a clinical setting, understanding the dying process is essential for healthcare professionals to provide comprehensive care and support to patients and their families during this critical period. A thorough understanding of the dying process can help clinicians address the physical, emotional, and spiritual needs of the patient while maintaining their dignity and comfort. To understand the dying process in a clinical setting, healthcare professionals can focus on the following aspects:

Identifying Signs and Symptoms

Clinicians should be knowledgeable about the common signs and symptoms that indicate a patient is nearing the end of life. These may include changes in vital signs, altered consciousness, increased restlessness or agitation, and irregular breathing patterns. By recognizing these signs, healthcare providers can better anticipate the patient's needs and adjust their care accordingly.

Communication and Education

Effective communication with the patient and their family is crucial during the dying process. Clinicians should provide clear and honest information about the patient's condition and prognosis, while also addressing any questions or concerns. Additionally, healthcare professionals should educate the patient's family on the dying process and what to expect, helping them prepare for the emotional and practical challenges ahead.

Pain and Symptom Management

In a clinical setting, it is essential to address any pain

or discomfort the patient may be experiencing. Healthcare professionals should closely monitor the patient's symptoms and collaborate with the palliative care team to ensure that they receive appropriate pain relief and symptom management interventions.

Emotional and Psychological Support

Healthcare providers should be aware of the emotional and psychological impact of the dying process on both the patient and their family. In a clinical setting, this may involve offering counseling services, providing spiritual care, or referring the family to relevant support groups or resources.

Interdisciplinary Care

The dying process often requires a collaborative approach from multiple healthcare professionals, including physicians, nurses, social workers, and chaplains. By working together, the interdisciplinary team can address the various needs of the patient and their family, ensuring that their care is well-coordinated and comprehensive.

Ethical considerations

As patients approach t he end of life, clinicians may

need to navigate complex ethical issues surrounding treatment decisions, such as the withdrawal of life-sustaining interventions or the administration of palliative sedation. Understanding the ethical principles involved in end-of-life care is crucial to ensure that patients' wishes are respected and their dignity is preserved.

By focusing on these aspects, healthcare professionals in a clinical setting can develop a deeper understanding of the dying process and provide compassionate, patient-centered care. This approach can help ease the physical and emotional burdens of the dying process, while also offering support and guidance to the patient's family during this challenging time.

When understanding the dying process and the principles of palliative care, healthcare providers, patients, and families can work together to create a compassionate and supportive environment during the final stages of life. This approach allows the patient to maintain their dignity and quality of life, while also providing comfort and solace for their loved ones.

Palliative care is a medical specialty that focuses on providing comfort, relief from pain, and support to individuals and their families who are facing life-limiting illnesses. Palliative care aims to improve the quality of life for individuals who are in the final stages of life, regardless of their diagnosis or prognosis. It is a holistic approach to care that addresses physical, emotional, social, and spiritual needs.

The dying process is a natural progression of life, and palliative care can help individuals and their families navigate this process with comfort and dignity. During this time, patients may experience a range of physical and emotional symptoms, and palliative care teams work to manage these symptoms and provide comfort.

In the final stages of life, individuals may experience changes in breathing and heart rate, a decrease in urination, and alterations in temperature. They may also experience changes in consciousness and a sense of detachment from family and friends. Some individuals may also experience a sense of disbelief or numbness and may see or hear departed loved ones.

As individuals approach the end of life, they may express a desire to put unfinished business in order, and many experience a sense of acceptance and peace. The goal of palliative care is to help individuals and their families through this process, providing comfort and support, and helping to create a peaceful and meaningful end of life experience.

In conclusion, the dying process and palliative care are important aspects of end-of-life care. Palliative care teams work to provide comfort and support to individuals and their families as they navigate the final stages of life, addressing physical, emotional, social, and spiritual needs.

Chapter 3
The Dying Process

When a person enters the end stages of the dying process, two different closely interrelated and interdependent dynamics are at work. The first dynamic is the physical process of the body shutting down. This is a natural process and is influenced by the individual's underlying medical condition, their age, and the presence of any other illnesses. The physical changes can be seen in the person's breathing, pulse, and body temperature.

The second dynamic is the emotional and spiritual experience of the person who is dying. This can be a time of reflection and contemplation, of letting go and finding peace. It can also be a time of fear, confusion, and uncertainty. The emotional and spiritual experiences of the person who is dying are influenced by their beliefs, values, and experiences throughout their life.

On the emotional and spiritual level, there is a *letting go* of life and a journey towards the unknown. This is a time when individuals often experience feelings of fear, sadness, and loss, as well as moments of peace and acceptance. It is important for loved ones and health care providers to be present and offer support, comfort, and dignity during this time. Whether it is through holding a hand, offering a listening ear, or providing a peaceful environment, being there for someone as they transition into the next phase of existence is a privilege and a testament to the deep connection that we all share as human beings.

At the same time, on the psychological and spiritual plane, the person is beginning a process of letting go of life and opening to the mystery of death. This can involve feelings of fear, sadness, anger, and acceptance, as well as experiences of peace, joy, and a sense of being held and supported by something greater than themselves.

It is important for the person and their loved ones to receive the support and care they need to navigate this delicate transition. Whether through medical treatment, spiritual practices, or simply being present with them. The goal is to help the person feel as comfortable and at peace as possible during this time of great change. In this way, the final stages of life can become a time of profound growth and transformation, not just for the person who is dying, but for those who love and care for them as well.

During this time, it is important for healthcare professionals and family members to be present and provide support for both the physical and emotional needs of the person who is dying. This may involve managing symptoms, providing comfort measures, and offering emotional support. It is a time of great vulnerability and sensitivity, but also a time of great meaning and purpose.

Emotional and Psychological Aspects

The emotional and psychological aspects of the dying process can be complex and challenging, both for the person who is dying and for those who are supporting them. As a person approaches the end of their life, they may experience a range of emotions, including fear, sadness, anger, and denial. These emotions can be difficult to manage, especially when the person is in physical pain or has limited mobility.

For those supporting the person who is dying, it is important to be aware of these emotional and psychological aspects of the dying process and to provide support and comfort. This may involve listening to the person's concerns, addressing their fears, and helping them to feel as comfortable as possible. In some cases, it may be appropriate to provide counseling or therapy to help the person process their emotions and come to terms with their impending death.

It is also important to remember that everyone's experience of the dying process is unique, and that what works for one person may not work for another. As such, it is important to be open and flexible, and to work with the person who is dying to develop a care plan that meets their individual needs and wishes.

Stages in the Dying Process

The dying process refers to the physical and psychological changes that occur in the body and mind as a person approaches death. The process of dying can be divided into several stages, although the exact timeline and symptoms can vary from person to person.

The Pre-Active Stage

The first stage of the dying process is called the *pre-active* dying stage. This is the stage in the dying process that occurs before the *active dying stage,* and is characterized by physical and psychological changes in the individual. The person may experience physical decline, increased fatigue or drowsiness, and decreased appetite and fluid intake. The body begins to slow down. These changes can be accompanied by psychological changes, such as confusion, restlessness, or agitation. This stage can last for weeks or months.

It is important to understand that the pre-active stage is a normal part of the dying process, and individuals and their loved ones should not be alarmed by these changes. However, it is important to be aware of these changes and to seek appropriate medical support if necessary.

The Active Stage

The second stage is called active dying. This is where the person's physical decline accelerates, and the body begins to shut down, and is a critical time in the dying process, and can be both physically and emotionally challenging for the individual and their loved ones. During this stage, the person may experience changes in breathing patterns, including shallow breaths, pauses in breathing, or a rattle-like sound. Their skin may become pale or mottled, decreased fluid and food intake, and they may become less responsive and more confused. During this stage, it is also important to provide emotional and psychological support to the individual and their loved ones. This may involve open and honest communication, providing a safe and comfortable environment, and encouraging meaningful connections with loved ones.

Emotionally, the individual may become more inwardly focused and detached from their surroundings, while their loved ones may experience feelings of sadness, fear, and uncertainty.

It's important to provide support and understanding during this stage and to acknowledge the individual's right to choose how they want to spend their final moments. Additionally, family, friends and care givers need to be aware of these changes and to provide appropriate support. This stage can last from several hours to several days.

The Post Death Stage
(Transition stage)

The final stage is called the *post-death* stage, in which the person has passed away, the body becomes still and begins to undergo physical changes that are associated with death.

In addition to physical changes, the dying process also brings with it emotional and psychological changes. People may experience fear, anxiety, and sadness as they approach the end of their lives. They may also experience a range of spiritual and existential questions and concerns. These emotions and experiences are normal and can be addressed through appropriate support and care.

It's also important to remember that this stage is a natural part of the dying process and that the individual is not in pain. In fact, their body may release chemicals that act like morphine to alleviate pain and cause sedation. At this time, it's important to provide comfort measures, such as maintaining a quiet and peaceful environment, to help the individual transition with dignity and peace.

During this time, it is common for the loved ones of the deceased to experience a range of emotions, including sadness, grief, and sometimes shock. This stage can be difficult, as the person is no longer physically present, and the reality of their loss can be overwhelming.

It is also important to take care of oneself during this time, as the grieving process can be physically and emotionally draining. Practicing self-care and reaching out to loved ones or support groups can help individuals navigate this stage.

Additionally, the post-death stage may involve making arrangements for the deceased, such as funeral planning and settling their affairs. This can be a challenging time, but it can also bring a sense of closure and a chance to celebrate the life of the person who has passed.

The post-death stage can be a challenging time, but it is important to allow oneself to grieve and to reach out for support when needed. By taking care of oneself and honoring the life of the deceased, individuals can find a path towards healing and moving forward.

Children and the Dying Process

The dying process can be a difficult and confusing time for children. It's important to be honest and open with them about what is happening, using language they can understand. Encouraging them to ask questions and share their feelings can also help them process their emotions and understand what is happening. It's also important to provide them with support, such as a trusted friend or family member, or a counselor, if needed. Allowing children to participate in the care of their loved one, in age-appropriate ways, can also help them feel involved and connected. It's important to remember that each child is unique and may respond differently to the dying process, and to be mindful of their individual needs and emotions throughout this time.

Children are often not fully equipped to understand death and can struggle to process their emotions and grief. It is important for parents, guardians, and caretakers to be open and honest with children about the dying process and to provide support and comfort throughout.

It is essential to keep in mind that children understand death and grieving differently based on their age and developmental stage. For example, younger children may have difficulty separating fantasy from reality, and may have trouble accepting that their loved one is truly gone. Older children may have more complex emotions, such as anger, guilt, or fear.

When approaching the topic with children, it is important to use age-appropriate language and to answer their questions truthfully. It is also helpful to give children a sense of control and comfort, such as allowing them to pick out special items for their loved one or to participate in memorial activities.

It is crucial to remember that children may experience grief differently than adults, and that their grieving process may last longer. It is important to provide ongoing support and resources, such as counseling or support groups, to help them through this difficult time.

Overall, it is essential to approach the dying process and the death of a loved one with sensitivity, compassion, and honesty when dealing with children.

Chapter 4
Physical Signs & Symptoms of The Dying Process ·

_____

Physical signs and symptoms of the dying process are a critical aspect of understanding the end-of-life journey. When a person is near death, their body experiences various changes that can be physical, emotional, and spiritual. These changes can be confusing and frightening for family members and loved ones who are present. Therefore, it is essential to have an understanding of what to expect so that you can offer comfort and support to your loved one during this time. Some of the physical signs and symptoms of the dying process include:

Changes in Breathing and Heart Rate

Changes in breathing and heart rate are physical signs

that a person may be entering the final stage of life. As death approaches and the body begins to shut down, it is not uncommon for breathing patterns may change. This can include shallow or irregular breaths or labored breaths, rapid breaths, or periods of no breathing at all. The heart rate may also become irregular or may slow down. These changes can be distressing for family members and loved ones, but it is important to understand that they are a natural part of the dying process.

Alterations in Temperature

You may notice the patient having changes in temperature - going from being hot and sweaty to cool and dry, and then to hot and dry. This is because the body's systems are shutting down, making it difficult to regulate the temperature. This is a natural process that occurs when changes in the chemistry of the body affect the body's temperature. It is important to provide comfort measures such as adjusting the room temperature or covering them with a lightweight blanket to keep them comfortable or lightly cover the patient with a sheet only, removing any blankets.

If necessary, administering acetaminophen can help lower the temperature, but it's important to consult with the Hospice nurse first, especially if the patient is unable to swallow medication. The nurse can help to determine the best course of action.

Changes in Skin Color and Temperature

Changes in skin color and temperature can be an indication of the progression of the dying process. This may occur due to a coolness in the hands, arms, and/or feet and legs that increases as their body begins to shut down. As a person nears death, their body temperature may drop, causing their skin to feel cool to the touch due to a decrease in circulation. Often accompanying the coolness are changes in color, where the lower part of the body becomes darker, and the skin may look blotchy or mottled. It's important to understand that these changes in temperature are normal and can be a sign that the end of life is near. In some cases, a person's skin may also take on a pale or yellowish hue.

These physical changes can be distressing for loved ones, but it's important to remember that they are a normal part of the dying process and should not cause undue alarm.

It's also important to provide comfort and support to the person during this time, as changes in skin color and temperature can make them feel uncomfortable or chilled. This can be done by using warm blankets, adjusting the temperature of the room, or providing skin-to-skin contact.

Your Hospice team is always available to provide support and guidance during this process.

Fatigue and Sleepiness

Fatigue and sleepiness are common physical symptoms experienced by individuals during the dying process. As the body begins to shut down, it can cause individuals to feel increasingly tired and have difficulty staying awake. This can be managed through the provision of comfort measures such as soft lighting, quiet surroundings, and comfortable bedding. It's important for family and caregivers to understand that this is a normal part of the dying process and to provide a peaceful and supportive environment to help the individual feel comfortable and at ease. Try to spend quality time with them when they are awake and rest when they are sleeping. Speak to them softly and naturally, even if they seem unresponsive, as hearing is often the last sense that remains. By providing a peaceful and comforting environment, you can help support your loved one during the dying process.

Additionally, it's important to address any discomfort or pain that may be contributing to the individual's fatigue and sleepiness, as this can have a significant impact on their quality of life during this time.

Decreased Appetite and Thirst

Decreased appetite and thirst are common symptoms near the end of life. As the body begins to shut down, the person may lose interest in eating and drinking. This can be due to physical changes in the body, such as difficulty swallowing, or changes in the person's energy levels and metabolism. Additionally, the person may feel full more quickly or have less of a desire to eat or drink. It's important to understand that this is a normal part of the dying process, and that it's not necessary to force feed or hydrate the person. Instead, focus on making them comfortable, and providing them with what they want and need to maintain their comfort and dignity. This may include soothing drinks, such as water or juice, or small, nutrient-rich snacks. Comfort measures, such as massages, can also help to relieve any physical discomfort they may be experiencing.

Decrease in Bodily Functions

During this stage, the body's energy and resources are being redirected to the internal organs, and the body is preparing for the final transition. As a result, many of the body's functions, such as digestion and elimination, slow down or stop. If your loved one is comfortable and pain-free, it is best to let nature take its course.

The decrease in bodily functions such as food and fluid intake and urinary output are normal during the dying process. The body is conserving energy and focusing on vital functions as the person nears the end of life.

Decreased urination is another common sign that a person is entering the final stages of life. As the body begins to shut down, it may become less efficient at eliminating waste, leading to decreased urination. This can also result in dehydration, which can cause discomfort and other symptoms. Understanding these changes and being prepared for them can help make this difficult time easier for both the person who is dying and their loved ones. Knowing the cause and purpose of these changes can also help alleviate any confusion or fear that may arise during this time. It is important to keep in mind that the medical team is always available to answer questions and assist with any concerns, and that comfort measures can be taken to help manage these symptoms.

During this time, family and loved ones should provide comfort measures and ensure that the person is as comfortable as possible during this time. This may include adjusting the bed to ensure a comfortable position, offering a cool cloth on the forehead, or simply holding the person's hand. It is also important to provide emotional support and be present for the person as they transition.

Incontinence

Incontinence refers to the loss of control over one's bladder and/or bowels. This can be a normal part of the dying process as the body begins to shut down and physical functions become less controlled. It can also be a side effect of certain medications or medical conditions. Incontinence can be distressing for both the patient and their loved ones, but it is important to remember that it is a natural part of the process and nothing to be ashamed of. To manage incontinence, it may be helpful to use incontinence products and to keep the patient clean and comfortable. It is also important to maintain privacy and dignity for the patient during this time.

Decreased Socialization

Decreased socialization during the dying process is a common symptom. As the body begins to slow down, it is common for individuals to withdraw from social activities and interactions. They may become less interested in engaging with others and may prefer to spend more time alone. This change in behavior can be difficult for loved ones to understand, but it is a natural part of the dying process.

It is important to remember that during this time, individuals are focusing their energy inward, and may be experiencing intense emotions and spiritual transformations. They may be saying goodbye to their loved ones in their own way and preparing for the next phase of their journey.

It is also important to provide comfort and support during this time, and to allow individuals to have the space and privacy they need. This may involve reducing stimulation, such as noise and bright lights, and allowing individuals to rest and sleep. Encouraging communication and providing a peaceful and loving environment can also be helpful in supporting individuals during this time.

Unusual Communication

Unusual Communication during the dying process refers to changes in the way a person communicates and interacts with the world around them as they approach the end of life. These changes can include shifts in the tone of voice, changes in the way the person communicates, and changes in the way they receive and process information.

During the dying process, individuals may experience physical, emotional, and spiritual changes that can affect their ability to communicate effectively. They may become more tired, confused, or disoriented, and may have difficulty articulating their thoughts and feelings.

It's important for caregivers and loved ones to be

aware of these changes and to approach communication with compassion and understanding. Simple gestures, such as holding the person's hand or speaking in a calm, soothing tone, can go a long way in helping to ease the dying person's anxiety and discomfort.

In addition, it's also important to recognize that the dying person may be communicating in non-verbal ways, such as through facial expressions or gestures. Caregivers and loved ones should be open to these forms of communication and work to interpret them in a way that provides comfort and support.

Overall, the dying process can be a time of great emotional intensity and spiritual transformation, and it's important to approach communication with sensitivity and care.

Changes in Consciousness

Changes in consciousness are a common occurrence during the dying process, and understanding these alterations can help healthcare professionals, patients, and their families better navigate this challenging time. As the body begins to shut down, the person may become increasingly drowsy or comatose. This can range from being more easily confused or disoriented, to being completely unresponsive. It is important to note that this is a natural part of the dying process and should not be seen as a sign of suffering. These shifts in consciousness can manifest in various ways, such as increased confusion, periods of unresponsiveness, or vivid dreams and visions.

In some cases, the person may become restless or agitated, or may start to mumble or talk in a way that is difficult to understand. This can be distressing for loved ones, but it is important to remember that it is a normal part of the process. It is also important to note that changes in consciousness can be affected by medications, so it is important to discuss any concerns with a medical professional.

It is important to remember that each person is unique, and the dying process can vary from one person to another, that these symptoms are not the same for everyone and may not occur in a particular order. However, understanding these common symptoms can help family members and loved ones provide the necessary support and comfort during this time. It's essential to understand that these physical changes are a normal part of the dying process, and that the person may be experiencing them in a way that is unique to them. Professional support resources, such as palliative care and hospice, can also be invaluable in helping with the physical and emotional needs of the dying person and their loved ones.

Chapter 5

Emotional, Spiritual, Mental Signs and Symptoms of Imminent Death

E motional-spiritual-mental signs and symptoms of imminent death are significant indicators of the final stages of life. These signs and symptoms reflect the internal changes that a person experiences as they approach death and can have a profound impact on their overall well-being. Understanding these changes is essential for providing appropriate care and support to the dying person and their loved ones.

When a person is nearing the end of their life, it is common for them to experience changes in their emotional, spiritual, and mental state. Some common emotional, spiritual and mental signs of imminent death include a sense of disbelief or numbness, seeing or hearing departed loved ones, expressing unfinished business, detachment from family and friends, and acceptance and peace. These changes can be difficult for loved ones to witness, but they are a natural part of the dying process and can indicate that the person is in a state of transition.

In terms of spiritual changes, a person may experience a heightened sense of spirituality or a deeper connection with their beliefs. This can bring comfort and peace in the face of death. On the other hand, they may also express fear or uncertainty about what happens after death.

It is important to provide emotional, spiritual, and mental support to the dying person and their loved ones during this time. This can involve active listening, offering comfort and support, respecting the person's wishes, and maintaining a positive attitude. Hospice and palliative care can also provide essential support for managing emotional and spiritual distress during the dying process. Some common emotional-spiritual-mental signs of imminent death include:

Withdrawal

The person may become less interactive with others, and may seem distant or unresponsive.

Confusion

The person may experience confusion or disorientation,

especially if they have cognitive decline.

Anxiety or agitation

The person may feel anxious, restless, or display signs of agitation.

Peacefulness

The person may become calmer and peaceful, and may seem to be at ease with their approaching death.

Spiritual or religious experiences

The person may express a sense of spiritual or religious connection, or have spiritual experiences, such as seeing or hearing things that are not there.

Hallucinations

The person may experience hallucinations or vivid dreams.

Acceptance

The person may express a sense of acceptance and peace with their approaching death.

It is important to understand that it is normal for these symptoms to fluctuate, and they may come and go over the course of the dying process.

A Sense of Disbelief or Numbness

A sense of disbelief or numbness is a common reaction during the end-of-life journey, an emotional response when facing the reality of death. This can occur when a person is unable to fully grasp the reality of the situation or feels emotionally detached from what is happening. This can be a defense mechanism as the mind tries to protect itself from the pain and trauma of loss.

People may feel as if they are in a state of shock or disbelief and may have difficulty accepting the reality of the situation. This response can be accompanied by feelings of numbness or detachment, as if the person is emotionally disconnected from what is happening. These feelings are normal. It is essential for individuals to seek support from loved ones and professional resources if they are feeling overwhelmed or unable to cope with these difficult emotions. To analyze the experience of disbelief or numbness, consider the following aspects:

Psychological defense mechanism

Disbelief or numbness can act as a psychological defense mechanism, allowing the individual to process the reality of their situation gradually. This emotional buffer can help protect them from the full impact of grief or distress, giving them time to adjust and come to terms with their new reality. Disbelief or numbness is also a natural part of the grieving process. It often occurs in the early stages of grief, when the individual is still processing the loss or impending loss. As the individual moves through the stages of grief, their emotions may shift and evolve, eventually leading to acceptance and healing.

Individual differences

The experience of disbelief or numbness can vary significantly from person to person. Factors such as personality, cultural background, and prior experiences with loss can all influence how an individual processes and copes with their emotions during this difficult time.

Supporting individuals in disbelief or numbness

Healthcare professionals and loved ones should approach individuals experiencing disbelief or numbness with patience, empathy, and understanding. It's essential to validate their feelings, offer a listening ear, and provide reassurance that their emotional responses are a natural part of the grieving process.

Encouraging healthy coping strategies

While disbelief or numbness can serve as a temporary coping mechanism, it's crucial to encourage individuals to explore and express their emotions in a healthy and supportive environment. This may involve connecting them with grief counseling, support groups, or other resources to help them process their feelings and work towards acceptance and healing.

Understanding the experience of disbelief or numbness in the context of loss and grief can help healthcare professionals and loved ones provide the necessary support and guidance during this challenging time. By acknowledging and validating these emotions, we can create a safe space for individuals to navigate their grief journey and find a path towards healing and acceptance.

Visions or Dream-Like Experiences

Visions or dream-like experiences are common near the end of life and are often viewed as a sign that the person is transitioning from this world to the next. During this time, the individual may see friends or family members who have passed away, or they may experience vivid, dream-like scenarios that provide comfort and peace. These experiences are not uncommon and can be a source of solace and comfort for both the dying individual and their loved ones.

It is essential to provide a supportive and non-judgmental environment that allows the dying individual to express their experiences freely, without fear of being dismissed or criticized.

While these experiences can be initially frightening, they are often a way for the person to prepare for the transition from this life to the next. The appearance of loved ones can provide comfort and reassurance to the individual as they prepare to transition from this life. The appearance of familiar and loved ones can help to make the transition less frightening and provide a sense of peace. These experiences can also serve as a way for the individual to make sense of their life and to process their emotions and thoughts as they approach the end of their life. It is important to be supportive and understanding of these experiences and to offer comfort and reassurance to the individual during this time.

It is important to understand that these experiences are not a hallucination or a side effect of drugs, but rather a natural part of the dying process. Understanding and accepting the uniqueness of each person's dying process can help to foster a peaceful and supportive environment for the individual and their loved ones during this difficult time.

Seeing or Hearing Departed Loved Ones

Seeing or hearing departed loved ones can be a common experience for some people during the dying process. This phenomenon is often referred to as *visions, visitations,* or *deathbed experiences.* It can bring comfort and peace to the dying person and those around them, as they may feel as though their loved ones are still with them. However, it's important to keep in mind that these experiences are subjective and can be influenced by a variety of factors, including medication, hallucinations, and cultural beliefs.

Regardless of their origin, these experiences can be powerful and meaningful for those who experience them, and it's important to offer support and understanding to the dying person and their loved ones.

Seeing or hearing departed loved ones is a phenomenon that some individuals experience during the dying process or while grieving the loss of someone close. These experiences can provide comfort, closure, or even spiritual insight for the individual, and understanding them can help healthcare professionals and loved ones offer support and validation during this challenging time.

To analyze the experience of seeing or hearing departed loved ones, consider the following aspects:

Prevalence of the phenomenon

Many individuals nearing the end of life or grieving the loss of a loved one have reported seeing, hearing, or feeling the presence of deceased family members or friends. These experiences, often referred to as deathbed visions or after-death communication, are relatively common and can provide a sense of reassurance and connection for the individual.

Emotional impact

For some, these encounters can offer comfort, solace, or a sense of closure, as they may feel reassured that their loved ones are watching over them or waiting for them on the other side. However, for others, these experiences may be unsettling or confusing, particularly if they are unsure of how to interpret them or if they conflict with their personal beliefs.

Cultural and spiritual perspectives

Cultural and spiritual beliefs play a significant role in shaping how individuals perceive and interpret these experiences. In some cultures or religious traditions, such encounters are seen as evidence of an afterlife or spiritual realm, while others may view them as a natural part of the grieving process or the brain's way of processing the loss.

Supporting individuals experiencing these phenomena

Healthcare professionals and loved ones should approach these experiences with sensitivity, empathy, and an open mind. It is important to validate the individual's experience, offer a listening ear, and provide reassurance without imposing one's own beliefs or interpretations.

Potential therapeutic benefits

For some individuals, discussing their experiences of seeing or hearing departed loved ones can provide an opportunity for emotional healing and personal growth. Encouraging open conversations about these encounters, either in a one-on-one setting or through support groups, can help individuals process their grief and find meaning in their experiences.

Understanding the phenomenon of seeing or hearing departed loved ones can help healthcare professionals and family members provide the necessary support and validation for individuals during the dying process or while grieving. By approaching these experiences with empathy and sensitivity, we can create a safe space for individuals to share their stories, explore their emotions, and find comfort and connection during this challenging time.

Expressing Unfinished Business

Expressing unfinished business refers to a common phenomenon that can occur as a person approaches the end of life. Unfinished business often refers to unresolved feelings, unspoken words, or unfulfilled desires that individuals may feel the need to address or reconcile before they can fully accept their circumstances and find peace. This can take many forms, such as talking about things they need to do or say or expressing a desire to see or speak to someone they have lost. These types of expressions can be a way for the person to feel a sense of peace and closure as they prepare to die.

This can be a confusing and a difficult experience for those around the person, who may not understand what is happening or why their loved one is making these statements. However, it is important to remember that these expressions are a normal part of the dying process and can be a way for the person to come to terms with their mortality.

It is helpful to listen to the person and acknowledge their feelings and expressions, as this can provide comfort and a sense of resolution in a time of great uncertainty. Additionally, it may be useful to offer support and reassurance, such as reminding the person of their accomplishments and the love of those around them.

In some cases, it may be appropriate to engage in practical or spiritual rituals to help the person feel a sense of completion or closure. This can include making plans for their funeral, writing letters to loved ones, or seeking spiritual guidance from a chaplain or religious leader.

To analyze the experience of expressing unfinished business, consider the following aspects:

Types of unfinished business

Unfinished business can take various forms, including unresolved conflicts, unexpressed feelings of love or gratitude, unsaid apologies, or unfulfilled dreams and aspirations. These unresolved issues can weigh heavily on an individual's mind and heart, potentially causing emotional distress or feelings of regret.

Importance of resolution

Addressing unfinished business can be an essential aspect of the grieving process or end-of-life journey, as it allows individuals to find closure, make amends, and come to terms with their emotions. Resolving unfinished business can promote emotional healing and contribute to a sense of peace and acceptance.

Encouraging open communication

Healthcare professionals and loved ones can support individuals in expressing their unfinished business by encouraging open, honest communication. Providing a safe and nonjudgmental environment for individuals to share their feelings, thoughts, and desires can help them work through unresolved issues and find closure.

Utilizing therapeutic interventions

In some cases, professional support may be needed to help individuals address their unfinished business. Therapeutic interventions such as counseling, grief therapy, or art and music therapy can provide a structured and supportive setting for individuals to explore their emotions, identify unresolved issues, and work towards resolution.

Spiritual and cultural considerations

Spiritual beliefs and cultural backgrounds can influence how individuals perceive and approach their unfinished business. Healthcare professionals and loved ones should be sensitive to these factors, offering support and guidance that respects and acknowledges the individual's unique beliefs and values.

Detachment from Family and Friends

Detachment from family and friends is a common sign and symptom of imminent death. As a person approaches the end-of-life, they may begin to withdraw from their loved ones and become less engaged with their surroundings. This emotional distancing may be a natural response to the complex emotions and changes associated with the dying process or the loss of a loved one. This can be due to a variety of physical and psychological factors, such as pain, fatigue, changes in consciousness, or a shift in focus towards inner thoughts and feelings.

For loved ones, this detachment can be difficult to understand and accept. It may feel like their loved one is pulling away from them, or that they are no longer interested in maintaining a relationship. However, this detachment is a normal part of the dying process and is not a reflection of how the person feels about their loved ones.

To help support a loved one during this time, it is important to be present, listen, and offer comfort. Encourage them to express their feelings and thoughts, and be patient if they need to be alone. Offer words of love and comfort and allow them to feel supported and cared for as they navigate this final stage of life. It can also be helpful to seek support from a hospice or palliative care team, who can provide guidance and resources to help you and your loved one cope with the changes that come with the dying process. To analyze the experience of detachment from family and friends, consider the following aspects:

Coping mechanism

Detachment may serve as a coping mechanism for individuals facing their own mortality or grappling with the loss of a loved one. By emotionally distancing themselves from their family and friends, individuals may be trying to protect themselves from the pain of separation or loss, allowing them to gradually process their emotions and come to terms with their new reality.

Energy conservation

As individuals approach the end of life, they may become physically and emotionally exhausted, leading them to withdraw from social interactions to conserve their energy. This detachment can be a natural part of the dying process, allowing the individual to focus on their inner journey and prepare for their transition.

Emotional protection for others

In some cases, individuals may detach from their loved ones as a means of shielding them from the emotional burden of their impending loss. By creating emotional distance, they may hope to ease their family and friends' pain and make it easier for them to cope with the eventual separation.

Supporting individuals experiencing detachment

Healthcare professionals and loved ones should approach individuals experiencing detachment with patience, empathy, and understanding. It's essential to respect their need for space and privacy while still offering a supportive presence and reassurance that they are loved and cared for.

Maintaining connections

Even when individuals withdraw from their social circles, it's important for family and friends to continue reaching out and providing emotional support. Maintaining connections through gentle touch, soft conversation, or simply sitting quietly with the individual can offer comfort and remind them that they are not alone.

Seeking professional help

If detachment becomes prolonged or significantly impacts an individual's quality of life, it may be helpful to seek professional guidance from a therapist, counselor, or support group. These resources can offer tailored support and coping strategies to help individuals navigate their emotions and reconnect with their loved ones.

Understanding the reasons behind this detachment can help healthcare professionals and loved ones provide appropriate support and guidance during this challenging time.

Acceptance and Peace

Acceptance and peace are often described as a state of mind or a feeling that can occur in the final stages of life. These qualities are essential emotional milestones for individuals nearing the end of life or coping with grief. They represent a state of emotional and psychological resolution, allowing individuals to come to terms with their circumstances and find a sense of inner harmony. During this time, the person may seem to have a greater sense of calm and contentment, despite the physical and emotional challenges they may be facing. This sense of peace can be a result of a number of factors, including acceptance of their illness, a resolution of any outstanding personal or emotional issues, and a sense of fulfillment or completion in life.

This experience of peace can be a comfort to both the person who is dying and their loved ones. It can also provide a sense of closure and help the individual to face death with dignity. However, it's important to note that not everyone will experience acceptance and peace in the final stages of life, and this can be due to various reasons such as fear of the unknown, unresolved emotional or spiritual issues, or a sense of unfinished business.

Regardless of whether or not acceptance and peace is achieved, it's important to provide supportive care for the person who is dying, including emotional support, comfort measures, and management of symptoms. This can help create a peaceful and comfortable environment for the person in their final days.

Understanding the journey towards acceptance and peace can help healthcare professionals and loved ones provide appropriate support and guidance during this critical time. To analyze the experience of acceptance and peace, consider the following aspects for stages of grief:

Acceptance

Acceptance is often considered the final stage of the grieving process, following denial, anger, bargaining, and depression. As individuals move through these stages, they gradually come to terms with their loss or impending loss, eventually reaching a state of acceptance and inner peace.

Emotional healing

The process of acceptance can be integral to emotional healing, as it enables individuals to acknowledge their circumstances and adapt to their new reality. Acceptance allows individuals to *let go* of resistance, relinquish the desire for control, and find solace in the present moment.

Personal growth

The journey towards acceptance and peace can also be an opportunity for personal growth and spiritual development.

By embracing the impermanence of life and the inevitability of loss, individuals may cultivate a deeper appreciation for the present moment, foster resilience, and develop a more profound sense of purpose and meaning.

Supporting individuals in finding acceptance and peace

Healthcare professionals and loved ones can support individuals in their journey towards acceptance and peace by providing a safe and nonjudgmental environment for them to express their emotions, offering a listening ear, and sharing comforting words or insights. Encouraging open communication, practicing empathy, and validating the individual's feelings can all contribute to their emotional healing and personal growth.

Therapeutic interventions

Various therapeutic interventions can help individuals find acceptance and peace, including grief counseling, support groups, mindfulness practices, and spiritual guidance. These resources can provide individuals with the tools and perspectives they need to navigate their emotions and foster a sense of inner harmony.

Understanding the journey towards acceptance and peace in the context of end-of-life care or grief can help healthcare professionals and loved ones provide the necessary support and guidance during this challenging time. By fostering open communication, offering emotional support, and encouraging therapeutic interventions, we can create a nurturing environment for individuals to process their emotions, heal, and ultimately find solace and peace in their circumstances.

Chapter 6

The Importance of Providing Appropriate Care

By gaining a deeper understanding of the dying process, healthcare professionals, family members, and caregivers can work together to provide compassionate, holistic care that addresses the needs of the individual and their loved ones. This can include managing pain, providing emotional and spiritual support, and respecting the wishes of the individual. By prioritizing understanding and empathy during the dying process, individuals and their loved ones can have a more peaceful and meaningful end-of-life journey.

Appropriate care is crucial in ensuring that individuals and their loved ones experience a peaceful and comfortable end-of-life journey. The dying process can be challenging and often includes physical, emotional, and spiritual changes, making it important to be prepared and informed. Providing appropriate care can involve a range of activities, from managing physical symptoms and discomfort to providing emotional and spiritual support. Each type of care should be rooted in compassion, dignity, and respect for the individual's journey towards the end of life.

Preserving dignity

Offering appropriate care ensures that individuals facing the end of life maintain their dignity. Dignity encompasses physical comfort, emotional well-being, and the ability to make choices about their care and surroundings. By providing compassionate and respectful care, we honor the inherent dignity of every person, regardless of their health condition.

Alleviating suffering

Palliative and end-of-life care aim to alleviate physical, emotional, and spiritual suffering. Pain management, symptom control, and psychosocial support are crucial components of appropriate care for the dying. By addressing these aspects, we help individuals find comfort and peace during their final days.

Fostering emotional support

Providing appropriate care involves supporting not only the

dying individual but also their loved ones. Family members and caregivers may experience profound grief, anxiety, and uncertainty as they navigate the end-of-life journey. Offering emotional support and guidance can help them cope with their feelings and find solace amidst the challenges.

Respecting autonomy

Respecting the autonomy of the dying individual means honoring their wishes and preferences regarding their care and end-of-life decisions. This may involve discussing and documenting advance directives, such as living wills and do-not-resuscitate orders, to ensure that their wishes are followed. By upholding autonomy, we empower individuals to have agency over their final days.

Promoting quality of life

Quality of life remains a central focus in end-of-life care. While cure may no longer be possible, enhancing the individual's quality of life through compassionate and holistic care is paramount. This may involve facilitating meaningful connections with loved ones, providing spiritual support, and creating a comfortable and peaceful environment.

Facilitating meaningful endings

Providing appropriate care allows individuals to experience meaningful endings tailored to their values, beliefs, and cultural practices. This may involve facilitating rituals, discussions about life's meaning and purpose, and opportunities for reconciliation and closure. By supporting individuals in crafting their own narratives, we honor the uniqueness of their life journey.

Honoring cultural diversity

It's essential to provide culturally sensitive care that respects the beliefs, traditions, and customs of the dying individual and their family. Cultural considerations can significantly influence end-of-life care preferences, rituals, and decision-making processes. By acknowledging and incorporating cultural diversity into care practices, we demonstrate respect for the individual's identity and values.

Supporting spiritual well-being

End-of-life care encompasses not only physical and emotional aspects but also spiritual dimensions. Many individuals find solace and comfort in their spiritual beliefs and practices as they approach death. Providing appropriate care involves addressing spiritual needs, such as facilitating discussions about faith, offering opportunities for prayer or meditation, and connecting individuals with spiritual support resources.

Facilitating communication

Effective communication is crucial in providing appropriate care to the dying. Open, honest, and compassionate communication helps individuals and their families navigate difficult conversations about prognosis, treatment options, and end-of-life preferences. It fosters trust, understanding, and collaboration among healthcare providers, patients, and families, ensuring that everyone is on the same page regarding care goals and decisions.

Promoting Comfort and Peace

At the end of life, comfort and peace become paramount goals of care. This involves managing pain and other distressing symptoms effectively, ensuring a serene and comfortable environment, and promoting a sense of emotional and existential peace. Palliative care specialists play a crucial role in addressing physical and psychological distress, allowing individuals to experience a peaceful and dignified transition.

Supporting family caregivers

End-of-life care extends beyond the dying individual to include their family caregivers, who often play a crucial role in providing support and comfort. It's essential to offer practical assistance, emotional support, and respite care to family caregivers, recognizing the physical, emotional, and spiritual toll of caregiving. Supporting caregivers helps alleviate their burden and ensures that they can continue to provide loving care to their dying loved ones.

In essence, providing appropriate care to the dying is not only a moral imperative but also a reflection of our shared humanity. It is an act of compassion, empathy, and reverence for the sacredness of life, even as it approaches its natural conclusion. By embracing the principles of dignity, comfort, autonomy, and support, we can ensure that every individual receives the compassionate care they deserve at the end of life.

In conclusion, providing appropriate care to the dying is a multifaceted endeavor that encompasses physical, emotional, spiritual, and cultural dimensions. It requires a holistic approach that honors the individual's dignity, respects their autonomy and preferences, addresses their physical and emotional needs, and supports their loved ones throughout the end-of-life journey. By embracing these principles, healthcare providers, caregivers, and communities can ensure that every individual receives compassionate and dignified care at the end of life.

By understanding the dying process and providing appropriate care, individuals and their loved ones can feel empowered and supported. This can lead to a more peaceful and comfortable experience, as well as a greater sense of closure and peace for those who have passed. Additionally, understanding the dying process and providing appropriate care can also help to reduce stress and anxiety for loved ones and caregivers, as they are better equipped to provide the support and comfort that is needed.

Chapter 7
Planes of Transition

Planes of transition refer to the different stages and dimensions that individuals may experience as they approach the end of their lives. This concept often encompasses physical, emotional, spiritual, and psychological aspects of the dying process. These stages can have a significant impact on the person's physical, emotional, and spiritual well-being, as well as their relationships with loved ones. It is essential to consider the varied experiences and perspectives that individuals and their loved ones may encounter during this transformative journey. It is important for those providing palliative care to understand these stages and to support the individual through them in a way that is meaningful and personalized to their needs and experiences.

To analyze the planes of transition, consider the following:

Physical plane

As individuals approach the end of their lives, they may experience a range of physical symptoms, such as changes in appetite, sleep patterns, energy levels, and pain. These physical manifestations can signal the progression of the dying process and require appropriate medical and palliative care interventions.

Emotional plane

The end-of-life journey can evoke a wide array of emotions, such as sadness, fear, anger, acceptance, and even relief. It is crucial for individuals and their loved ones to acknowledge, express, and process these emotions as they navigate the planes of transition.

Spiritual plane

Individuals may seek solace, meaning, and comfort in their spiritual beliefs or philosophical views during the end-of-life journey. This plane of transition may involve contemplating one's place in the universe, the afterlife, or the interconnectedness of all living beings.

Psychological plane

The psychological aspects of the end-of-life journey can

include coming to terms with one's mortality, reflecting on one's life accomplishments and regrets, and finding a sense of closure or acceptance. This plane of transition can also involve addressing any unresolved issues or unfinished business.

Relational plane

As individuals approach the end of their lives, they may experience a shift in their relationships with loved ones, friends, and caregivers. This plane of transition can involve expressing gratitude, forgiveness, love, and farewells, as well as seeking closure and reassurance.

Death is a natural part of life, and the way in which we approach it can have a significant impact on the dying person and their loved ones. It is important to recognize that there are both physical, emotional-spiritual-mental-relational aspects to the dying process. The two processes of the physical and emotional-spiritual-mental-relational aspects of dying are intertwined and complementary. Understanding the physical and emotional-spiritual-mental changes that may occur can help us better prepare and provide comfort and support to our loved ones during this challenging time.

The physical changes that occur as the body prepares to shut down are a normal and natural part of the process and can be addressed through comfort-enhancing measures. On the other hand, the emotional, spiritual, mental, and relational changes that occur as the spirit prepares to release from the body and all attachments, can be supported through responses that encourage and facilitate this release and transition, a supportive and encouraging environment. Ultimately, these two processes should be approached in a way that is appropriate and unique to the values, beliefs, and lifestyle of the dying person. Allowing the dying person to have control and make choices in their final moments can greatly impact the peace and comfort they experience.

The following listings of physical, emotional, psychological, spiritual, and relational signs and symptoms of imminent death are offered to help you understand the natural occurrences during the dying process and how you can respond appropriately. The timing and sequence of events can vary greatly. However, having an understanding of these changes that may occur can help you provide comfort and support to the dying person and their loved ones.

Physical Plane

On the physical plane, the body begins to shut down as its systems cease to function. This process is not a medical emergency and requires comfort-enhancing measures. The spirit of the dying person begins to release itself from the body, its environment, and all attachments. Usually this is an orderly and un-dramatic progressive series of physical changes. Such changes are not medical emergencies and do not require invasive interventions. However, these physical changes can be accompanied by physical symptoms that can cause discomfort, such as pain, restlessness, difficulty breathing, and others. It's important for healthcare providers to manage these symptoms and ensure the comfort of the dying person.

The dying process is a time of transition, and it's important to provide care and support to the person who is dying and their loved ones. This can include managing physical symptoms, providing emotional and spiritual support, and honoring the person's wishes and preferences. By doing so, we can help ensure that the dying process is as peaceful and dignified as possible. These physical changes are a normal, natural way in which the body prepares itself to stop. The most appropriate kinds of responses are comfort-enhancing measures.

As the body begins the final stages of shutting down, it is a natural and normal process that should be respected and supported by those around the person. Comfort-enhancing measures, such as providing a peaceful and comfortable environment, reducing pain and discomfort, and offering emotional support, are the best ways to respond to the physical changes during this time. By focusing on comfort and support, we can help make this final stage of life as peaceful and dignified as possible.

The signs and symptoms mentioned are only offered to help you understand the changes that may happen and how you can respond in the most appropriate way. It is essential to keep in mind that not all of these signs will show up with every person, and they may not occur in a particular sequence. Each person's journey through death is individual and personal, and it is essential to respect and honor their unique path.

Emotional Plane

The other dynamic of the dying process at work is on the emotional-spiritual-mental plane and this is a different kind of process. The emotional-spiritual-mental plane of the dying process is a time for personal reflection, for coming to terms with life, and for letting go. It is a time for finding meaning and closure, for seeking resolution and for finding peace. This inner journey is a deeply personal and individual experience, and one that may be enhanced by the support of family, friends, and spiritual care providers. During this time, it is important for individuals to be given the space and support they need to explore their feelings, beliefs, and desires. Whether through quiet contemplation, conversation with loved ones, or spiritual practices, the emotional and spiritual aspects of the dying process can provide comfort, healing, and a sense of inner peace. In this way, the two dynamics of the dying process, the physical and the emotional-spiritual-mental, work together to support the individual as they transition from life to death.

On the emotional and spiritual plane, people often reflect on their life, relationships, and values. They may experience a range of emotions, such as fear, sadness, anger, or acceptance. They may also have spiritual or existential questions. It's important for family members and healthcare providers to be attentive to these emotional and spiritual needs and provide support and comfort during this time.

The spirit of the dying person begins the final process of release from the body, its immediate environment, and all attachments. This emotional-spiritual-mental process is different from the physical process in that it is a time of letting go, of release, and of transition from one state of being to another. The dying person may experience a range of emotions, including fear, confusion, anger, sadness, and peace, as they face this final journey. It is important for loved ones and care providers to support the dying person in this process, by providing comfort and love, and by helping them to feel safe and at peace as they transition. This can involve listening to their needs, honoring their wishes, and providing emotional and spiritual support. By being present and attentive to their needs, care providers can help the dying person to move through this process with as much peace and comfort as possible.

The most appropriate kinds of responses to the emotional-spiritual-mental changes are those which support and encourage this release and transition. This includes providing an atmosphere of comfort, safety, and peace, and being present to listen, offer love and reassurance, and to simply be there for the person while providing reassurance and validation, and allowing time and space for the dying person to express their feelings and experiences. It is also important to honor their wishes and respect their autonomy, respect the individual's beliefs and spirituality, and to provide any resources or rituals that may be helpful for them during this time. The process of letting go and transitioning can be a time of great peace, release, and resolution, and it is important to support and facilitate this process in the most gentle and loving way possible. This approach recognizes the dignity and sacredness of the dying process and supports the person in their final journey towards death.

The team of caring professionals wants the friends and family to know what to expect as death approaches, so that it may seem less frightening. This understanding can bring comfort to them and allow them to be more present and supportive during this time of transition. The goal is to provide love, comfort, and support, and to allow the natural process to unfold in its own time. This requires understanding of what is happening and what you can do to support your loved one.

It is important to be patient and compassionate, and to offer comfort and understanding as they go through this final stage of life. By providing this kind of support, you can help your loved one to feel at peace and to have a sense of dignity and comfort as they make this transition. Remember, this is a time to show your love and to be there for them, offering whatever support and comfort you can.

Psychological Plane

The psychological plane refers to the mental and emotional aspects of an individual's experience, including their thoughts, feelings, and beliefs. It encompasses the individual's sense of self, their relationships, and their life experiences. In the context of the dying process, the psychological plane can play a significant role in shaping an individual's experience and their understanding of what is happening to them. This includes the individual's perception of their illness and their prognosis, their level of hope, their coping strategies, and their relationships with others. It is important for healthcare providers to understand the psychological plane and its impact on the dying process in order to provide appropriate care and support to individuals and their families. This may involve providing emotional support, addressing psychological and spiritual needs, and helping individuals and their families to make sense of their experiences.

Spiritual Plane

The spirit of the dying person begins the final process of release from the body, its immediate environment, and all attachments. As the dying person embarks on this journey, their spirit begins to detach from their physical body, the environment around them, and any emotional or mental connections they have to the world. This process is unique to each individual and can follow its own priorities and timeline.

This release also tends to follow its own priorities. For some, resolving any unresolved issues or "unfinished business" may be a priority during this time. This can be practical matters such as settling their affairs or making amends with people they may have hurt. For others, the focus may be more spiritual or emotional, such as finding peace and acceptance, or seeking closure.

Regardless of what each person prioritizes during this process, it is important to recognize that it is a normal, natural part of the journey of dying, and one that can bring a sense of peace and closure. Comfort-enhancing measures, such as providing a peaceful and supportive environment, can help support the dying person during this time.

The resolution of these matters can bring a sense of peace and closure, allowing the person to *let go* of their physical body with greater ease. It is important for healthcare professionals to be aware of these emotional and spiritual dynamics and to provide support and resources to assist with the resolution of unfinished business, if desired. This can help to create a more peaceful and harmonious transition for the dying person and their loved ones.

It is a common belief that the dying person must resolve these unfinished matters before they can fully release their spirit. This idea stems from the understanding that unresolved issues, be it emotional or relational, may prevent an individual from finding peace and acceptance during their final moments. As loved ones gather around, offering support and comfort, they often engage in meaningful conversations to help the dying person find closure and reconciliation. This process of resolving unfinished matters can be deeply healing for both the dying person and their loved ones, allowing them to say their goodbyes and express their love, gratitude, and forgiveness.

By addressing these unresolved matters, the dying person can release any lingering burdens, fears, or regrets, and ultimately, allow their spirit to transition with a sense of peace and completion. This profound experience not only eases the dying process but also provides solace and understanding for those left behind, as they too come to terms with the inevitable loss.

This process is not always obvious or apparent to those around them, but it is a deeply personal and meaningful experience for the person who is dying. It is important for loved ones to provide a supportive and non-judgmental environment during this time, to allow the dying person to resolve their unfinished business in their own way and in their own time. The focus should be on comfort and dignity, rather than trying to control or manipulate the process. This release process is a profound and transformative journey, and the support of those around them can make a significant difference in the experience of the dying person.

Receiving permission to *let go* from family members is often an important part of this release. The process of letting go may involve accepting that death is near, expressing feelings, and resolving any unresolved issues. It may also involve saying goodbye and receiving forgiveness or giving forgiveness to others. This process can be both peaceful and transformative for the dying person and for those who are close to them. By acknowledging and addressing the emotional, spiritual, and mental aspects of dying, individuals are able to find peace and closure in their final moments.

These events are the normal, natural way in which the spirit prepares to move from this life into the next dimension of existence. These events are often experienced by the dying person as a journey or a process of transition. The support of loved ones, family members, and medical professionals can make this transition easier and more peaceful. Understanding the dynamics of the dying process can help the dying person and their loved ones to better cope with the changes that are taking place, and to provide comfort and support during this time.

This is a crucial moment in the life of your loved one, and the focus should be on their comfort and well-being, rather than trying to alter the situation or change their experience. This is not the time to try to change your loved one, but the time to give full acceptance, support, and comfort.

During the final stages of life, it is important to be there for your loved one, to listen to their needs and provide them with the comfort and support they require. By offering acceptance, support, and comfort, you can help to create a peaceful and positive atmosphere that will ease their transition and provide them with the care and comfort they need during this time. This is a time for empathy, love, and understanding, and to create a peaceful and comfortable environment for your loved one. This is a time for loving presence, for holding space, and for being there for your loved one in their time of need.

As no two people will experience death in exactly the same way, and there is no right or wrong way to approach this final stage of life. It is important to be open and understanding of the differences that exist, and to provide support and comfort to the person who is dying in a way that feels appropriate and meaningful to them.

By helping someone through this process, you are offering them the greatest gift of love imaginable. Providing comfort, support and understanding during the final stage of life can bring peace and closure to both the dying person and their loved ones. It is a selfless act of love and compassion that will leave a lasting impact on all those involved. Whether through physical touch, emotional comfort, or simply being present, being there for a loved one during this time can bring immense comfort and ease to both the dying person and their family.

Please remember that your medical team is always available to answer questions, assist you with any concerns, and make a personal visit. This is a reminder that you are not alone in this process and that there are trained professionals who are dedicated to helping you and your loved one during this time. It is important to reach out and ask for help when needed, as the team is there to provide comfort, support, and guidance.

Relational Plane

The relational plane refers to the emotional and social relationships that individuals have with others during the dying process. This plane encompasses the connections and interactions between the individual who is dying, their family members and friends, and their healthcare providers. The relational plane is important in palliative care as it provides a sense of comfort, support, and connection to the individual who is dying.

During this time, individuals may have a heightened need for affection, love, and connection with those they care about. Maintaining strong relationships with loved ones can provide comfort, hope, and a sense of purpose during the dying process. Healthcare providers can play a key role in supporting the relational plane by creating a welcoming and supportive environment, encouraging open communication, and creating opportunities for families to spend time with their loved one.

The relational plane is also significant as it can impact the emotional and psychological well-being of the individual who is dying, as well as their family members and friends. By providing support and comfort through relationships, individuals can feel less isolated, lonely, and anxious during the dying process.

In conclusion, understanding the different planes of transition and the goals of palliative care can help individuals and families navigate the end-of-life journey with greater ease and grace. By acknowledging the emotional and spiritual aspects of the dying process and providing appropriate care and support, we can help those who are facing this challenging time to find peace, comfort, and dignity.

Chapter 8

**Supporting Loved Ones During
The Dying Process**

Supporting loved ones during the dying process can be a challenging and emotional experience. It is important to understand the physical and emotional changes that may occur during this time, as well as the goals of palliative care and the holistic approach to care. This can help individuals provide support that is tailored to the specific needs of their loved one, and can help to promote comfort, dignity, and peace in their final days.

Supporting loved ones during the dying process is a crucial and challenging aspect of palliative care. It can be difficult to see someone you care about suffer and go through the physical, emotional, and spiritual changes that come with the dying process. However, it is important to provide support and comfort to those who are suffering, as well as their family and friends.

One key aspect of supporting loved ones during the dying process is to be present and available to them. This can involve listening to their needs and concerns, and offering comfort and support as needed. This can involve simply being present, holding their hand, and listening to their needs and concerns. You can also provide emotional support by talking to them, sharing memories, and letting them know that they are not alone. It may also involve providing practical assistance with daily activities, such as bathing or eating, or managing symptoms such as pain or fatigue.

In terms of practical support, you can help with activities of daily living, such as bathing, eating, and dressing. You can also help manage pain and symptoms by working with the hospice team and advocating for your loved one's comfort and care.

In addition, it is important to consider the emotional and spiritual needs of individuals during this time. This may involve having conversations about their beliefs and values, or simply offering a listening ear and a supportive presence. It may also involve providing access to religious or spiritual resources, such as a chaplain or spiritual advisor, or simply being available for quiet moments of reflection or meditation.

It is also important to take care of yourself during this

time. This can mean seeking support from friends and family, as well as seeking professional counseling if necessary.

Ultimately, the goal of supporting loved ones during the dying process is to promote comfort, dignity, and peace in their final days. This can involve advocating for their needs and wishes, and working with healthcare providers to ensure that their care is in line with their goals and values. It may also involve supporting them through the grieving process, and being there for them as they adjust to life without their loved one. By providing compassionate and supportive care, individuals can help their loved ones to experience a peaceful and dignified passing and can support them as they navigate this difficult and emotional journey.

Supporting loved ones during the dying process can be a challenging experience for everyone involved. It is important to remember that each person's experience is unique and to approach it with sensitivity and empathy. The following are some ways to support your loved one during this time:

Being Present

Being present is a vital component of providing compassionate and meaningful support to individuals nearing the end of life or coping with grief. By practicing active listening, nonverbal communication, emotional availability, and mindfulness, healthcare professionals, family members, and friends can create a nurturing environment that fosters connection, healing, and solace during this challenging time.

Spend time with your loved one and let them know that you are there for them. Being present during the dying process can be a challenging and emotional experience, but it can also be incredibly rewarding. By being present, you are showing your love and support for them during one of the most difficult times in their life. It is important to remember that everyone grieves differently and there is no right or wrong way to do it. You can start by simply being there for your loved one, listening to them, and offering comfort. This may involve holding their hand, providing a hug, or simply being a shoulder to lean on.

Being present, both emotionally and physically, is an essential aspect of supporting individuals nearing the end of life or coping with grief. It involves giving your full attention and focus to the individual, their emotions, and their needs, allowing them to feel seen, heard, and valued. Understanding the importance of being present can help healthcare professionals, family members, and friends provide the most meaningful and compassionate support during this difficult time. To analyze the concept of being present, consider the following aspects:

Active listening

Being present involves actively listening to the individual, paying close attention to their words, emotions, and body language. This is a crucial part of supporting a loved one as it allows them to express their thoughts and feelings and can provide a sense of comfort and validation. This attentiveness can help you better understand their needs, concerns, and feelings, allowing you to provide more effective support and validation.

When someone is facing the end of their life, they may have many thoughts and emotions that they want to share. Allowing them to do so without judgment by providing a safe space where they feel free to share their experiences, can help them feel heard and understood. Listening can also provide a sense of connection, which can be especially important during this difficult time. By simply being present and offering an ear to listen, you can make a big difference in your loved one's experience.

Listening can help to reduce feelings of isolation and loneliness and provide comfort and support during a difficult time. When someone is dying, it is natural for them to feel anxious, scared, and overwhelmed. By simply being present and offering a listening ear, you can help to ease their fears and provide emotional support. This kind of active listening can be a powerful tool in helping someone through the dying process and can have a profound impact on their emotional well-being.

Nonverbal communication

Nonverbal cues, such as maintaining eye contact, offering a gentle touch, or simply sitting quietly with the individual, can convey a sense of presence and support. These actions can help create a safe and nurturing environment, where the individual feels comfortable sharing their thoughts and emotions.

Encourage open communication

Encourage open and honest communication about their experiences and feelings.

Emotional availability

Being present also requires emotional availability, meaning that you are open and receptive to the individual's emotions without becoming overwhelmed or overly reactive. Keeping emotional balance allows you to remain grounded and focused on the individual's needs, providing a steady and supportive presence.

Prioritizing quality time

Making an effort to spend quality time with the individual, without distractions or competing demands, can help you be more fully present with them. This focused attention can help deepen your connection and provide a more meaningful and supportive experience. Spending quality time together can help build memories and provide comfort. Share stories, laugh, and simply be present in the moment.

Recognizing the value of presence

Sometimes, simply being present with the individual, without offering solutions or advice, can be the most powerful form of support. Recognizing that your presence can provide comfort, validation, and a sense of connection can help you better appreciate the value of this aspect of caregiving.

Provide comfort

You can also provide emotional comfort by simply being there and offering support. Offering physical comfort through touch or holding hands can also be positively impactful to one facing the uncertainty of their inevitable transitioning.

Offer practical help

Offer to run errands, cook meals, or help with other tasks. You can also help by providing practical support, such as helping with household chores or running errands. It is important to be patient and understanding as allowing your loved one to see otherwise may negate your efforts.

Celebrate their life

Share memories and celebrate the life of your loved one.

Mindfulness and self-awareness

Practicing mindfulness and self-awareness can help you stay present and focused during emotionally challenging situations. By cultivating an awareness of your own emotions, thoughts, and physical sensations, you can maintain a calm and centered state, better equipped to support the individual in their end-of-life journey or grieving process.

Seek support

It is important to take care of your own well-being, so reach out to friends, family, or support groups for help and support. Remember to take care of yourself too, as the grieving process can be difficult for everyone involved.

It is important to remember that the dying process is a natural part of life, and to approach it with compassion and understanding. Providing support to a loved one during this time can be a deeply meaningful experience and a way to show your love and care.

Offering Comfort and Support

When a loved one is going through the dying process, it can be an emotional and difficult time for both the person who is dying and their family and friends. Offering comfort and support to a loved one during this time is not just about doing the right thing, but also about being there for them. This is a crucial part of the grieving process and can provide immeasurable comfort during this difficult time.

Offering comfort and by understanding the emotional, physical, and spiritual needs of the individual and their loved ones, healthcare professionals, family members, and friends can help create a nurturing environment that fosters healing and solace during this challenging time. involve a variety of different actions and behaviors, including:

The power of touch

Touch is an important form of comfort and support. Holding your loved one's hand, gentle touches like a hug, a kiss on the forehead or a pat on the arm can provide physical and emotional comfort.

Reading to them

If your loved one is unable to speak or read, you can read to them. This can be anything from a book, poem, or even the newspaper.

Providing a peaceful environment

A calm and peaceful environment can provide comfort to

your loved one. Dim the lights, play soothing music, and keep the room quiet and free from distractions..

Emotional support

Providing emotional support involves validating the individual's feelings, offering a listening ear, and sharing comforting words or insights. Encouraging open communication and creating a safe, nonjudgmental space can help individuals process their emotions and feel understood.

Physical comfort

Attending to the individual's physical comfort is an essential aspect of offering support. This may involve managing pain, addressing symptoms, ensuring proper hygiene, and creating a comfortable and soothing environment, adjusting their pillows, providing a warm blanket or offering a drink of water. Being attentive to the individual's physical needs can significantly contribute to their overall well-being and quality of life.

Spiritual support

Addressing spiritual concerns and offering spiritual support can be an integral part of providing comfort during the end-of-life journey or grieving process. This may involve discussing existential questions, connecting the individual with spiritual leaders or resources, or offering prayer, meditation, or other spiritual practices as appropriate.

Practical assistance

Offering practical support, such as helping with daily tasks, organizing finances, or coordinating care, can alleviate some of the burdens faced by the individual and their family. This assistance can help create a more manageable and supportive environment during this challenging time.

Presence and companionship

Sometimes, the simple act of being present and offering companionship can provide significant comfort and support. Spending quality time with the individual, engaging in meaningful activities, or simply sitting quietly together can create a sense of connection and shared experience.

Support for loved ones

Offering comfort and support to the individual's family members and friends is also essential, as they may be grappling with their own emotions and challenges. Providing emotional support, practical assistance, or simply a listening ear can help loved ones navigate their grief and caregiving responsibilities.

Offering comfort and support to individuals nearing

the end of life or coping with grief is a vital aspect of compassionate care. By addressing emotional, physical, and spiritual needs, and providing practical assistance and companionship, healthcare professionals, family members, and friends can create a nurturing environment that fosters healing, connection, and solace during this challenging time.

Respecting Wishes

Respect your loved one's privacy and give them space if they need it. Respecting someone's privacy during the dying process is an important aspect of supporting them. It can be a difficult and emotional time for everyone involved, but it's crucial to ensure that the patient's wishes are honored and respected. This can include respecting their physical space, avoiding intrusions into their personal life, and avoiding conversations or activities that they may find uncomfortable.

It's also important to be mindful of the impact of your words and actions on the patient and their loved ones. Avoiding intrusive questions or comments and being mindful of the patient's physical and emotional needs, can help create a supportive and peaceful environment for everyone involved.

By respecting the privacy of the person who is dying, you are allowing them to have a sense of control and dignity during what can be a vulnerable time. You are showing that you care about their needs and well-being and are allowing them to have a peaceful and comfortable journey towards the end of their life. This also means allowing them to have private moments and conversations with loved ones, and not invading their personal space.

It is also important to respect their wishes regarding medical treatments and interventions. For example, if they do not want to be resuscitated or put on a breathing machine, it is important to respect their decision.

Respecting a person's wishes a crucial aspect of palliative care. It's also important to respect a person's spiritual and emotional needs during this time. This might mean accommodating religious or cultural practices, or simply being there to listen and provide comfort. By respecting a person's wishes, you can help ensure that their last days are spent with dignity and comfort, surrounded by loved ones who support them. This can also help provide a sense of peace and closure for both the person who is dying and their loved ones. To analyze the concept of respecting wishes, consider the following aspects:

Communication and understanding

Open communication and a clear understanding of the individual's wishes are crucial in ensuring that their preferences are respected. Engaging in honest conversations about their needs, values, and beliefs can help healthcare professionals, family members, and friends collaborate more effectively to provide the best possible care.

Advance care planning

Encouraging the individual to engage in advance care planning, including creating advance directives or designating a healthcare proxy, can help ensure that their wishes are respected in various medical situations. This proactive approach can provide clarity and guidance for healthcare professionals and loved ones during decision-making processes.

Cultural and spiritual considerations

Respecting the individual's cultural and spiritual beliefs is essential in providing compassionate care. This may involve accommodating religious practices, rituals, or dietary restrictions, as well as acknowledging the role of faith and spirituality in the individual's experience of illness and grief.

Involvement in decision-making

Including the individual in decision-making processes, whenever possible, can help ensure that their wishes are respected and their voice is heard. This involvement can range from discussing treatment options to making choices about their daily care and routines.

Supporting autonomy and dignity

Respecting the individual's wishes often involves supporting their autonomy and dignity, even as their physical or cognitive abilities decline. By acknowledging their right to make choices and maintain control over their lives, healthcare professionals, family members, and friends can help preserve the individual's sense of self and identity.

Flexibility and adaptability

Respecting wishes may require flexibility and adaptability, as the individual's preferences and needs may change over time or in response to their evolving condition. Being open to revisiting conversations and adjusting care plans as needed can help ensure that the individual's wishes continue to be respected throughout their end-of-life journey or grieving process.

Respecting the wishes of individuals nearing the end of life or coping with grief is a vital aspect of compassionate care. By fostering open communication, supporting autonomy and dignity, and being adaptable to changing needs and preferences, healthcare professionals, family members, and friends can work together to create a nurturing environment that honors the individual's values, beliefs, and desires during this challenging time

Maintaining a Positive Attitude

Maintaining a positive attitude during the end of life journey can be a challenging task, but it is important to keep in mind that this time is about being present and supportive for the person who is dying. Keeping a positive attitude can help the person feel more at ease and provide comfort to both the person and those around them.

A positive attitude can take many forms, including maintaining a hopeful outlook, focusing on the good memories and times, and finding joy in small moments. It can also involve being open-minded and respectful of the person's wishes and choices, additionally being patient and understanding when things do not go as planned.

It is important to remember that everyone copes with death differently, and that maintaining a positive attitude may look different for each person. The most important thing is to be present and supportive for the person who is dying, and to offer comfort and love during this difficult time.

It is important to approach the end-of-life journey with empathy, compassion, and understanding, and to focus on what can be done to help the person who is dying to feel comfortable and at peace. This may involve engaging in activities that the person enjoys, providing physical comfort, or simply being present and offering support.

Maintaining a positive attitude during the end-of-life journey or when coping with grief is essential for both individuals facing these challenges and their loved ones. A positive mindset can help create a more supportive environment, foster resilience, and promote emotional well-being during difficult times. By understanding the importance of maintaining a positive attitude, healthcare professionals, family members, and friends can work together to provide compassionate care and encouragement. To analyze the concept of maintaining a positive attitude, consider the following aspects:

Focus on the present moment

Encouraging mindfulness and a focus on the present moment can help individuals and their loved ones appreciate the time they have together and find joy in small moments. This practice can promote a positive outlook and enhance overall well-being.

Cultivate gratitude

Fostering a sense of gratitude for the experiences, relationships, and memories shared can help individuals and their loved ones maintain a positive perspective during difficult times. Reflecting on the blessings and positive aspects of life can offer a sense of balance and hope.

Seek emotional support

Accessing emotional support from friends, family, support groups, or professional counselors can help individuals and their loved ones navigate the challenges of the end-of-life journey or grieving process. Sharing feelings and receiving encouragement can foster a more positive mindset and promote resilience.

Engage in meaningful activities

Participating in activities that bring joy, meaning, or a sense of accomplishment can help individuals and their loved ones maintain a positive attitude during challenging times. These activities may include creative pursuits, hobbies, or spending quality time with loved ones.

Foster a sense of purpose

Encouraging individuals to explore their sense of purpose and identify meaningful goals can contribute to a more positive outlook. This may involve reflecting on their legacy, engaging in acts of service, or focusing on personal growth and development.

Practice self-compassion

Cultivating self-compassion and extending kindness and understanding to oneself can help individuals and their loved ones maintain a positive attitude during difficult times. Recognizing that everyone's experiences challenges and imperfections can foster a more gentle and supportive perspective.

Maintaining a positive attitude during the end-of-life journey or when coping with grief is a crucial aspect of promoting emotional well-being and resilience. By focusing on the present moment, cultivating gratitude, seeking emotional support, and engaging in meaningful activities, healthcare professionals, family members, and friends can work together to create a nurturing and supportive environment that fosters hope, connection, and healing during challenging times.

Encourage Open Communication

Encourage open and honest communication about your loved one's experiences and feelings. This means creating a safe, non-judgmental and supportive environment where your loved one feels comfortable sharing their thoughts, feelings, and experiences with you. Open communication can help the person to express their needs, fears, and concerns and feel heard and validated. It can also provide an opportunity for loved ones to share their own feelings and provide support. This can help them feel heard, understood, and validated, which can bring a sense of peace and comfort during a difficult time.

To encourage open communication, it's important to be an active listener and to avoid judgment or criticism. You can also ask open-ended questions and express genuine interest in what they have to say. Additionally, it's important to give your loved one the space and time they need to talk, without feeling rushed or pressured.

Remember that everyone experiences the dying process differently and that everyone has their own unique way of communicating. By encouraging open communication, you can help your loved one feel seen, heard, and supported as they navigate this challenging time.

Seeking Support for Yourself

When supporting a loved one during the end-of-life journey, it is important to also take care of oneself. Seeking support can help individuals manage their own emotions and stress levels. This can be done through a variety of means such as talking to friends and family, participating in support groups, or seeing a counselor.

It is also important to engage in self-care activities such as exercise, mindfulness, and hobbies that bring joy. This can involve reaching out to friends and family for support, seeking therapy, or joining a support group. It is important to address any feelings of grief, stress, or anxiety and to take care of oneself in order to be able to provide the best support possible for the loved one during this difficult time.

Taking breaks from caregiving and allowing oneself to rest and recharge can also be crucial in maintaining one's own well-being. Remember, it is okay to feel overwhelmed and to ask for help. Seeking support is a sign of strength and can help individuals maintain their own physical and emotional health while supporting their loved one through this difficult time.

Seeking support for yourself while providing care or companionship to someone nearing the end of life or coping with grief is essential for maintaining your own emotional well-being and resilience. By recognizing the importance of self-care and accessing available resources, you can better navigate the challenges and emotions that arise during this difficult time. To analyze the concept of seeking support for yourself, consider the following aspects:

Recognize your own emotions

Acknowledging and validating your own feelings is a crucial first step in seeking support. By being honest with yourself about your emotions, you can better understand your needs and identify the appropriate resources or coping strategies.

Reach out to friends and family

Sharing your thoughts, feelings, and experiences with close friends or family members can provide a valuable source of emotional support and encouragement. These connections can help you feel understood, validated, and less alone in your journey.

Access professional support

Seeking professional guidance from therapists, counselors, or spiritual advisors can offer additional emotional and mental support during challenging times. These professionals can provide tools and insights to help you cope with the emotions and stressors you may be facing.

Join a support group

Connecting with others who are experiencing similar situations can provide a sense of understanding and camaraderie. Support groups can offer a safe space for sharing experiences, emotions, and coping strategies while fostering a sense of community and connection.

Practice self-care

Prioritizing self-care, including engaging in activities that bring you joy and relaxation, can help maintain your emotional well-being and resilience. Make time for hobbies, exercise, meditation, or other activities that help you feel refreshed and recharged.

Set boundaries

Establishing and maintaining boundaries can help you balance your caregiving responsibilities with your own well-being. Communicate your limits and needs to others and allow yourself the time and space to recharge and tend to your own emotional and physical health.

Accessing respite care

Respite care provides temporary relief for caregivers, can offer a valuable opportunity for rest and rejuvenation. This support can help you maintain your own well-being while ensuring that your loved one continues to receive the care they need.

Seeking support for yourself while providing care or companionship to someone nearing the end of life or coping with grief is vital for maintaining your own emotional well-being and resilience. By recognizing your emotions, reaching out to friends, family, and professionals, and prioritizing self-

107

care, you can better navigate the challenges and emotions that arise during this difficult time. By taking care of yourself, you'll be better equipped to provide the compassionate support and care that your loved one needs.

Celebrate Their Life

Celebrating someone's life is a meaningful way to honor their memory and the impact they had on the world around them. This can take many forms, from creating a photo album of cherished memories to organizing a memorial service to simply sharing stories and reflections with friends and family. Celebrating a loved one's life can also help those who are grieving to find comfort and solace in their memories, and to feel connected to the person they have lost.

It is important to remember that everyone grieves in their own way, and there is no right or wrong way to celebrate someone's life. Some people find solace in religious or spiritual rituals, while others prefer to focus on the person's hobbies and interests. Some people find comfort in large, public gatherings, while others prefer more intimate, private celebrations.

Ultimately, the most important thing is to find a way to celebrate the life of your loved one that feels authentic and meaningful to you. Whether it's through a public memorial service, a small gathering of close friends and family, or simply by reflecting on their life in your own way, honoring their memory is an important step in the grieving process and helps to ensure that their legacy lives on.

Celebrating the life of a loved one who is dying is an important and meaningful way to honor their memory and pay tribute to all the things they accomplished, experienced and meant to those around them. This can be done through various means, such as sharing stories, making a scrapbook, displaying photos, or creating a memory jar. It can be a way for friends and family to come together and remember the life that has been lived and the impact it has had on their lives.

Celebrating a life can help bring closure, comfort, and peace during a difficult time, allowing individuals to focus on the positive memories and experiences they shared with their loved one. It is also a way to show love and appreciation for the person, even in their passing.

It's important to acknowledge that everyone grieves differently and there is no right or wrong way to celebrate a life. What is important is that the process is meaningful and helps bring comfort to those who are grieving.

In conclusion, celebrating the life of a loved one who has passed is a powerful way to show love, honor their memory, and bring comfort during a difficult time. It is a way to celebrate the positive moments, acknowledge their impact, and pay tribute to their legacy.

Chapter 9
Grief and Bereavement

Grief is a normal and natural response to loss, and it is a complex and often overwhelming experience. It is a journey that affects all aspects of a person's life, including their thoughts, feelings, behaviors, and relationships. While grief can be incredibly difficult, it is important to remember that it is a temporary experience and that it is possible to heal and move forward.

However, it is important to understand that grieving is a process, and that it is possible to heal and move forward. This may involve seeking support from friends, family, or a mental health professional, as well as engaging in self-care activities such as exercise, mindfulness, and journaling.

It is also important to be kind and patient with oneself during this time, and to understand that the grieving process takes time. With support and self-care, it is possible to heal and find a new sense of meaning and purpose in life after loss. The process of grieving can be long and difficult, but with time and support, it is possible to come to terms with the loss and find a new normal.

Grief and bereavement are natural and complex emotional responses to the loss of a loved one. These experiences can be marked by a wide range of emotions, including sadness, anger, guilt, and disbelief. By understanding the various aspects of grief and bereavement, individuals, healthcare professionals, family members, and friends can better navigate these emotional journeys and provide compassionate support during difficult times.

Coping Strategies

Developing healthy coping strategies, such as journaling, creative expression, exercise, or meditation, can help individuals navigate their grief and build resilience. Encouraging the exploration of various coping techniques can empower individuals to find the methods that best support their healing process.

Long-Term Healing

Grieving is a long-term process that may evolve over time but never truly ends. Individuals may experience waves of grief or find that their emotions shift as they adapt to their new reality. Acknowledging the ongoing nature of grief can help individuals cultivate patience and self-compassion as they continue to heal and grow.

It is important to practice self-care during the grieving process and to seek support from friends, family, or professional resources when necessary. Grief can also be affected by cultural and religious beliefs, and it is important to be mindful of these differences and to offer support that is respectful of these beliefs.

For children and adolescents, grief can be especially challenging, as they may not have the emotional or developmental maturity to understand what is happening. It is important to support children during their grief journey and to help them to understand the process and to find healthy ways to cope with their feelings.

Understanding the Grief Process

The grief process is a natural reaction to loss and can involve a wide range of emotions, physical symptoms, and changes in behavior. It is a unique experience for each individual and can last for different periods of time, ranging from weeks to years and in some cases a lifetime. The process typically involves several stages, including shock and disbelief, anger, bargaining, depression, and acceptance. It is important to remember that grief is not a linear process, and individuals may experience these stages in a different order or revisit certain stages multiple times.

Grief can be triggered by many types of loss, including death, divorce, or the loss of a job. It is a normal response to loss and is not something that can or should be "fixed" or "cured." Rather, it is a process of adapting to a new reality and finding a new way to move forward in life.

It is important to seek support and engage in self-care during the grieving process. This can include talking to friends or family members, seeking support from a counselor or therapist, or participating in support groups. It is also important to be kind to yourself and to give yourself permission to grieve in your own way and at your own pace.

Understanding the grief process is also essential for individuals, healthcare professionals, family members, and friends who are navigating the complex emotional journey that follows the loss of a loved one. By recognizing the various stages and experiences of grief, we can provide compassionate support and help foster healing during this challenging time. To analyze the concept of understanding the grief process, consider the following aspects:

Grief stages and models

Many models have been developed to describe the stages of grief, with one of the most well-known being the Kübler-Ross model, which includes denial, anger, bargaining, depression, and acceptance. It is important to remember that these stages may not occur in a linear fashion and individuals may experience them in their own unique order or even revisit certain stages.

Individual experiences

Each person's experience of grief is unique and may be influenced by factors such as their relationship with the deceased, their cultural background, their coping strategies, and their support network. Recognizing the individuality of grief can help us approach each person's journey with empathy and understanding.

Emotional reactions

Grief can manifest in a wide range of emotions, including sadness, anger, guilt, disbelief, relief, or even moments of happiness. Validating these emotions and providing a safe space for their expression can facilitate the grieving process.

Physical symptoms

Grieving individuals may experience physical symptoms such as fatigue, sleep disturbances, appetite changes, or headaches. Understanding the connection between grief and physical well-being can help guide appropriate support and self-care measures.

Coping strategies

Encouraging the exploration of various coping strategies, such as journaling, creative expression, exercise, or meditation, can empower individuals to find the methods that best support their healing process. Providing resources and guidance on coping techniques can facilitate growth and resilience during the grieving process.

Support networks

Building and maintaining strong support networks, including friends, family, support groups, or professional counselors, can play a vital role in the grieving process. These connections can offer understanding, encouragement, and a safe space for sharing emotions and experiences.

Time and patience

Acknowledging the non-linear and ever-evolving nature of grief can help individuals cultivate patience, self-compassion, and understanding as they navigate their emotional journey.

Understanding the grief process is crucial for providing compassionate support and fostering healing for individuals experiencing the loss of a loved one. By recognizing the various stages, emotional reactions, and coping strategies associated with grief, we can approach each person's journey with empathy, understanding, and patience. This knowledge can empower us to create a supportive environment that nurtures growth, resilience, and healing during this challenging time.

Common Reactions to Grief

Common reactions to grief can be varied and complex, as each individual experiences the loss of a loved one in their own unique way. By recognizing and understanding these common reactions, we can better support those who are grieving, validate their emotions, and encourage the healing process. To analyze and narrate common reactions to grief, consider the following:

Emotional reactions

Grief can evoke a wide range of emotions, including sadness, anger, guilt, disbelief, relief, loneliness, or even moments of happiness. It is essential to validate these emotions, as they are all natural parts of the grieving process.

Physical symptoms

Grieving individuals may experience physical symptoms such as fatigue, sleep disturbances, appetite changes, headaches, or digestive issues. Recognizing the connection between grief and physical well-being can help guide appropriate support and self-care measures.

Cognitive reactions

Grief can also impact cognitive functioning, leading to difficulties in concentration, memory, or decision-making. Being aware of these cognitive changes can help individuals and their support network navigate these challenges with patience and understanding.

Behavioral reactions

People experiencing grief may exhibit behavioral changes, such as withdrawing from social activities, engaging in repetitive or ritualistic behaviors, or seeking comfort in familiar routines or environments. Recognizing these behaviors can provide insight into an individual's coping strategies and emotional state.

Spiritual reactions

Grief can lead to questions about one's faith, beliefs, or the meaning of life, and may prompt a reevaluation of personal values or spiritual practices. Offering support and understanding for those experiencing spiritual struggles can provide comfort and guidance during this challenging time.

Relational reactions

Grieving individuals may experience changes in their relationships with others, such as feeling disconnected, seeking increased support, or experiencing conflict. By acknowledging the impact of grief on relationships, we can better support and understand the evolving dynamics during the grieving process.

Emotional triggers

Grieving individuals may encounter emotional triggers, such as anniversaries, holidays, or reminders of their loved one. Being aware of these triggers can help individuals and their support network prepare for and navigate the emotions that may arise.

Common reactions to grief are varied and complex, encompassing emotional, physical, cognitive, behavioral, spiritual, and relational aspects. By recognizing and understanding these common reactions, we can better support those who are grieving, validate their emotions, and encourage the healing process. Providing empathy, understanding, and patience can help create a supportive environment that fosters growth, resilience, and healing during this challenging time.

Healthy Ways to Cope with Grief

Healthy ways to cope with grief can include a variety of activities and strategies that help a person process their emotions, connect with others, and take care of themselves. Some common healthy coping mechanisms include:

- Talking to a trusted friend or family member about your feelings.

- Writing in a journal or creating art to express your emotions.

- Engaging in physical activity, such as going for a walk or doing yoga.

- Seeking support from a therapist or grief support group.

- Practicing mindfulness and relaxation techniques, such as deep breathing or meditation.

- Focusing on self-care, such as eating well, getting enough sleep, and engaging in activities that bring you joy.

- Finding meaning through volunteer work or other activities that give back to the community.

It is important to remember that everyone grieves differently and there is no one "right" way to cope with grief. What works for one person may not work for another, so it is important to try a variety of strategies and find what works best for you.

Coping with grief is a deeply personal and individual process. However, there are several healthy ways to cope with grief that can provide comfort, support, and healing during this challenging time. By exploring and engaging in these healthy coping strategies, individuals experiencing grief can build resilience and find solace in their emotional journey. To analyze healthy ways to cope with grief, consider the following:

Acknowledge and express emotions

Encourage individuals to acknowledge their emotions and express them openly, whether through talking, writing, or creative outlets. Emotional expression can provide relief, validation, and insight into the grieving process.

Seek support

Encourage individuals to seek out support from friends, family, support groups, or professional counselors. A strong support network can provide understanding, encouragement, and a safe space for sharing emotions and experiences.

Self-care

Encourage grieving individuals to prioritize self-care by maintaining a healthy diet, getting regular exercise, and ensuring adequate rest. Focusing on physical well-being can help promote emotional resilience and overall health.

Establish routines

Encourage individuals to establish or maintain routines that provide structure and a sense of normalcy during the grieving process. Daily routines can help individuals feel grounded and connected to their lives.

Engage in meaningful activities

Encourage individuals to engage in activities they find meaningful, such as volunteering, pursuing hobbies, or spending time in nature. Meaningful activities can help individuals find purpose and connection during their grieving process.

Allow time for grieving

Encourage individuals to give themselves time and space to grieve, recognizing that the process is unique to each person and may not follow a linear timeline. Patience and self-compassion can be invaluable during this time.

Develop healthy coping strategies

Encourage individuals to explore and develop healthy coping strategies, such as meditation, journaling, artistic expression, or mindfulness practices. These strategies can help individuals navigate their grief and build emotional resilience.

Seek spiritual support

Encourage individuals to explore their spirituality or beliefs, if they find it helpful. Seeking spiritual support can provide comfort and guidance during the grieving process.

Honor the deceased

Encourage individuals to honor their loved one by engaging in rituals, creating memorials, or sharing memories. Honoring the deceased can provide a sense of connection and meaning in the grieving process.

Reach out for professional help

If grief becomes overwhelming or impacts daily functioning, encourage individuals to seek professional help from a therapist, counselor, or bereavement specialist. Professional support can provide additional guidance and resources during the grieving process.

Healthy ways to cope with grief can provide comfort, support, and healing for individuals experiencing the loss of a loved one. By exploring and engaging in these healthy coping strategies, individuals can build resilience and find solace in their emotional journey. Encouraging the use of these strategies can create a supportive environment that fosters growth, resilience, and healing during this challenging time.

Unhealthy Ways to Cope with Grief

Unhealthy ways to cope with grief include suppression, denial, avoidance, substance abuse, escaping reality, and anger.

It's important to recognize that unhealthy coping mechanisms may bring temporary relief, but they can ultimately hinder the healing process and lead to additional problems. It's important to find healthy and constructive ways to cope with grief, such as talking to a friend or therapist, engaging in physical activity, or finding a support group.

While grieving is a deeply personal and individual process, it is crucial to recognize and avoid unhealthy coping strategies that may hinder healing and emotional well-being. Understanding these unhealthy ways to cope with grief can help individuals and their support networks recognize potential pitfalls and redirect toward healthier alternatives. To analyze unhealthy ways to cope with grief, consider the following:

Suppressed emotions

Bottling up emotions or not expressing them can result in emotional stagnation, increased stress, and potentially explosive emotional outbursts down the road.

Denial or avoidance

Refusing to accept the reality of the loss or avoiding the grieving process may provide temporary relief, but it can hinder long-term healing and lead to unresolved emotions.

Substance abuse

Turning to alcohol or drugs as a means of numbing emotions or escaping from the pain of grief is an unhealthy coping mechanism that can have lasting negative consequences on physical and emotional well-being.

Excessive isolation

While it's natural to seek solitude during the grieving process, withdrawing entirely from social interactions and support systems can exacerbate feelings of loneliness and depression.

Overworking

Immersing oneself in work or other activities to the point of neglecting self-care and emotional processing can lead to burnout and prevent healthy grieving.

Over-identifying with the deceased

Losing oneself in the identity or memories of the deceased to the point of neglecting one's own needs and personal growth can hinder the ability to move forward in life.

Unresolved anger or guilt

Dwelling on feelings of anger or guilt without addressing or processing them can perpetuate negative emotions and impede healing.

Unhealthy rumination

Continuously replaying the events surrounding the loss or obsessing over "what-ifs" can reinforce feelings of helplessness and prolong the grieving process.

Neglecting self-care

Ignoring physical, emotional, and spiritual needs during the grieving process can exacerbate feelings of sadness and prolong healing.

Developing compulsive behaviors

Engaging in compulsive behaviors, such as excessive cleaning or hoarding, as a means of coping with grief can be unhealthy and unproductive in the long term.

By recognizing and avoiding these unhealthy coping strategies, individuals experiencing grief and their support networks can redirect towards healthier alternatives that promote growth, resilience, and healing. Offering understanding, patience, and support can help create a nurturing environment for those navigating the grieving process.

Coping with Special Occasions and Anniversaries

Special occasions and anniversaries can be particularly difficult for those who are grieving. These events can trigger strong emotions and memories of the person who has died, making it hard to focus on anything else. It's important to find healthy ways to cope with these difficult times. Some ways to cope include reaching out to friends and family, participating in memorial activities, or finding alternative ways to celebrate the occasion. It's also important to be gentle with yourself and allow yourself to feel your emotions, whether that means crying or taking time for self-care. Additionally, it's okay to modify traditions or create new ones that feel more meaningful and comfortable. The most important thing is to do what feels right for you and what helps you through the difficult time.

By understanding and implementing healthy coping strategies, individuals can navigate these occasions with greater ease and resilience. To analyze coping with special occasions and anniversaries, consider the following:

Plan ahead

Anticipate the emotions that may arise during special occasions and anniversaries, and create a plan for how to handle them. This may include seeking support, engaging in self-care, or setting boundaries with social engagements.

Create new traditions

Developing new traditions or adapting old ones can provide a sense of continuity and comfort while also honoring the memory of the deceased. This might involve visiting a special place, preparing a favorite meal, or engaging in an activity that the deceased enjoyed.

Seek support

Reach out to friends, family, or support groups for understanding, encouragement, and companionship during special occasions and anniversaries. Surrounding oneself with people who are aware of the emotional significance of the event can provide a sense of connection and shared experience.

Set realistic expectations

Acknowledge that special occasions and anniversaries may be difficult and give oneself permission to experience a range of emotions without judgment. Setting realistic expectations can help minimize feelings of guilt or disappointment if the day does not unfold as hoped.

Honor the deceased

Find ways to honor the memory of the deceased during special occasions and anniversaries. This might involve lighting a candle, sharing memories and stories, or creating a tribute to celebrate their life.

Prioritize self-care

Make self-care a priority during special occasions and anniversaries by ensuring proper nutrition, rest, and relaxation. Engaging in activities that promote emotional well-being, such as exercise, meditation, or journaling, can also be helpful.

Allow for flexibility

Be open to adjusting plans or traditions as needed, recognizing that emotions and needs may change from year to year. Flexibility can help create space for growth and healing.

Focus on gratitude

Reflect on positive memories, personal growth, and the support received from others during the grieving process. Focusing on gratitude can help create a sense of perspective and appreciation for the journey of healing.

Seek professional help if needed:

If special occasions and anniversaries trigger overwhelming emotions or feelings of despair, consider seeking professional help from a therapist, counselor, or bereavement specialist. They can provide additional guidance and support during these challenging times.

Coping with special occasions and anniversaries can be challenging for those grieving the loss of a loved one. By understanding and implementing healthy coping strategies, individuals can navigate these events with greater ease and resilience. Offering understanding, patience, and support can help create a nurturing environment for those experiencing grief during these emotionally significant times.

Chapter 10
Grief in Different Cultures and Beliefs

Grief is a universal human experience, but the way it is expressed and experienced can vary greatly among different cultures and beliefs. Cultural and religious beliefs can shape the way people view death and the grieving process and can influence the types of rituals and customs that are performed to honor the dead. It's important to be mindful of these cultural differences and to respect the beliefs and practices of others during the grieving process.

For example, in some cultures, the grieving process is seen as a time to come together as a community and offer support to one another, while in others it is a time to withdraw and be alone. Some cultures may have specific rituals, such as ancestor veneration or the creation of memorials, that are used to help the bereaved process their loss. Religious beliefs can also play a role, with some people finding comfort in prayer, meditation, or other spiritual practices, while others may feel a sense of detachment from their faith during this time.

By understanding and respecting these cultural and religious differences, we can offer support to those who are grieving in a way that is meaningful and appropriate for them. To analyze grief in different cultures and beliefs, consider the following:

Mourning rituals and customs

Different cultures have unique rituals and customs surrounding death and mourning. These practices can include specific burial rites, periods of mourning, and rituals to honor the deceased. Understanding these customs can provide valuable insight into the cultural significance of grief and the ways it is managed within a specific context.

Grieving process

The grieving process can vary across cultures, with some emphasizing the expression of emotions, while others may focus on stoicism or acceptance. It is essential to recognize that there is no universally "correct" way to grieve and that cultural variations in the grieving process are deeply rooted in tradition and belief systems.

Spiritual beliefs

Spiritual beliefs surrounding death, the afterlife, and the role of the deceased in the lives of the living can greatly influence how grief is experienced and processed. Understanding these beliefs can help provide a framework for interpreting and supporting the grieving process within different cultural contexts.

Social support and community involvement

The role of social support and community involvement in the grieving process can vary widely across cultures. Some cultures may emphasize the importance of collective mourning and community support, while others may place greater value on individual or family-based grieving practices.

Expression of grief

Cultural variations in the expression of grief can include differences in mourning attire, physical displays of emotion, and the use of art, music, or other forms of creative expression. Understanding these cultural nuances can help create a supportive environment that respects and acknowledges the diverse ways in which grief can be expressed.

Role of gender and age

Cultural expectations around gender and age can influence

the grieving process. In some cultures, specific roles and expectations may be placed upon individuals based on their gender or age, which can shape their grieving experience.

Grief is a complex and deeply personal experience that is influenced by a wide range of cultural and spiritual beliefs. By exploring and understanding the diverse ways in which grief is experienced and processed across different cultures, we can foster empathy, promote cross-cultural understanding, and create a supportive environment for those navigating the grieving process. This understanding can help us better support friends, family members, and colleagues as they experience grief within the context of their cultural background and belief system.

Cultural Differences in Grieving

Cultural differences in grieving refer to the way different cultures, communities, and societies approach the process of mourning and bereavement. The beliefs, values, rituals, and customs surrounding death and loss can vary widely between cultures, affecting the way individuals experience and cope with grief.

For example, some cultures place a strong emphasis on communal grieving, with large public gatherings and rituals to honor the deceased. Other cultures may prioritize more private mourning, with a focus on individual reflection and spiritual connection. Some cultures have strong religious beliefs that shape the way they understand death and the afterlife, while others may have a more secular perspective.

Cultural differences in grieving reflect the diverse ways in which societies process and express grief. These variations can be seen in mourning rituals, social support, spiritual beliefs, and emotional expression. Recognizing and understanding these differences can foster empathy and support for those experiencing grief from diverse cultural backgrounds. To analyze cultural differences in grieving, consider the following:

Mourning rituals

Cultures often have unique mourning rituals that serve to honor the deceased and provide a structured framework for grief. For example, some cultures may emphasize specific burial practices or hold ceremonies to commemorate the deceased. Understanding these rituals can help us appreciate the cultural context of grieving.

Social support

The role of social support in grieving can vary across cultures. In collectivist societies, grieving might be a community-centered process, whereas in individualistic societies, grief may be considered a more private experience. Recognizing these differences can help us offer appropriate support to those from diverse cultural backgrounds.

Spiritual beliefs

Spiritual beliefs surrounding death and the afterlife can greatly impact how grief is experienced and processed. Some cultures believe in reincarnation or ancestral spirits, while others might emphasize the concept of heaven or another form of afterlife. These beliefs can shape the grieving process and may offer comfort and hope to those who are mourning.

Emotional expression

Cultural norms around emotional expression can influence how grief is experienced and shared. Some cultures might encourage the open expression of emotions, while others may promote restraint or stoicism. Understanding these cultural variations can help us create a supportive environment for those who grieve in different ways.

Timeframes for mourning

Different cultures have varying expectations around the duration of mourning. In some cultures, a specific period of mourning is observed, whereas, in others, there may be no set timeframe. Respecting these cultural differences can help us offer support in a manner that aligns with the bereaved person's cultural context.

Gender roles and expectations

Cultural expectations around gender can also impact the grieving process. In some cultures, men and women may be expected to grieve differently or assume different roles within the grieving process. Recognizing these expectations can help us better understand and support those navigating grief within their cultural context.

The Impact of Religious Beliefs on Grief

Religious beliefs play a significant role in how individuals grieve and cope with loss. For many people, their faith provides comfort and a sense of hope during a difficult time. However, the way in which religious beliefs impact grief can vary greatly depending on the individual's culture and religion. To analyze the impact of religious beliefs on grief, consider the following:

Perspectives on death and the afterlife

Different religions offer diverse perspectives on death and the afterlife, which can significantly influence the grieving process. Beliefs in heaven, reincarnation, or ancestral spirits can provide comfort and hope for those who are grieving, shaping their understanding of the meaning and purpose of death.

Mourning rituals and practices

Religious beliefs often inform specific mourning rituals and practices, which can serve as a structured framework for processing grief. These may include funeral ceremonies, prayer, or meditation, which can offer solace and a sense of connection to the deceased or a higher power.

Emotional expression and coping mechanisms

Religious beliefs may provide guidance on how emotions should be expressed or managed during the grieving process. Some faith traditions may encourage the open expression of grief, while others may promote acceptance or detachment. Understanding these differences can help us better support those grieving within their faith tradition.

Community and social support

Many religious communities provide valuable social support for those who are grieving, offering a sense of connection and shared understanding. Participation in religious services, support groups, or other community gatherings can help individuals navigate their grief within a supportive and nurturing environment.

Meaning-making and personal growth

Religious beliefs can offer a framework for making sense of loss, helping individuals find meaning and purpose in their grief. This may involve the belief that the deceased is now in a better place, that their spirit continues to exist in some form, or that their death serves a greater purpose within the context of their faith.

Coping through faith

For many individuals, their religious beliefs can be a source of strength and comfort during the grieving process. Prayer, meditation, or engaging in religious rituals can provide a sense of connection to a higher power, which can be a valuable coping mechanism in times of loss.

The impact of religious beliefs on grief can be multifaceted, can vary greatly, and deeply personal. For many individuals, their faith provides a source of comfort and a sense of hope during a difficult time. By recognizing and understanding and respecting the ways in which religious beliefs shape the grieving process, we can offer empathetic and informed support to those who are mourning within the context of their faith tradition. This understanding allows us to be more sensitive and compassionate when offering support and guidance to friends, family members, and colleagues as they navigate the complexities of grief and loss within their unique religious contexts.

Grief in Children and Adolescents

Grief can be a difficult and overwhelming experience for anyone, but it can be especially challenging for children and adolescents. Unlike adults, children may not fully understand what is happening and why they are feeling the way they are. They may not know how to express their emotions, and they may not have a developed support system.

It is important to understand that children may grieve differently than adults, and that their reactions can vary depending on their age, developmental stage, and individual personality. For example, young children may have difficulty understanding death and may have a tendency to ask repetitive questions. They may also experience physical complaints or exhibit behavioral problems, such as tantrums or sleep disturbances. Adolescents may struggle with feelings of guilt and anger, and may have difficulty trusting others or forming relationships.

It is important for adults to provide support to children during this difficult time. This may include listening to them, being patient, and answering their questions as honestly as possible. It is also important to involve children in the grieving process by allowing them to attend funerals or memorial services, if they choose to, and encouraging them to express their feelings through activities such as drawing, writing, or talking.

In some cases, children may benefit from counseling or therapy to help them process their grief. This can provide a safe space for them to talk about their emotions and can help them work through their feelings in a healthy way.

Grief in children and adolescents can manifest differently than in adults due to their unique developmental stages and emotional understanding. It is essential to recognize and address the specific needs and experiences of grieving children and adolescents to provide appropriate support and guidance. To analyze grief in children and adolescents, consider the following:

Developmental understanding of death

Children's and adolescents' comprehension of death is influenced by their cognitive and emotional development. Younger children may not fully grasp the permanence of death, while older children and adolescents may have a deeper understanding. This developmental perspective can shape their grieving process and the type of support they need.

Emotional expression

Children and adolescents may express their grief differently than adults. They may display a range of emotions, such as anger, confusion, fear, or sadness. It is crucial to acknowledge and validate these emotions and create a safe space for them to express their feelings.

Regression and behavioral changes

Grieving children and adolescents may exhibit changes in behavior, such as regression to earlier developmental stages, sleep disturbances, or changes in appetite. Recognizing these behaviors as potential manifestations of grief can help caregivers provide appropriate support and understanding.

Coping strategies

Children and adolescents may employ various coping strategies to deal with their grief, such as engaging in creative activities, play, or seeking comfort from familiar routines. Encouraging and supporting healthy coping mechanisms can help them navigate their grief.

Peer support and social connections

Friendships and social connections can be a significant source of support for grieving children and adolescents. Encouraging them to maintain these connections and providing opportunities for peer support can be beneficial during the grieving process.

Age-appropriate communication

Communicating about death and grief with children and adolescents should be done in an age-appropriate manner, using language that they can understand. This may involve using stories, metaphors, or simplified explanations to help them grasp complex concepts related to death and loss.

Professional support

In some cases, children and adolescents may benefit from professional support, such as counseling or therapy, to help them process their grief. Some organizations offer and organize camping experiences as a safe and scared place for children and adolescents to experience "good grief" as a therapeutic strategy. This can provide them with additional tools and resources for coping with their loss.

Understanding grief in children and adolescents requires recognizing the unique ways in which they experience and process loss. By acknowledging their developmental perspectives, emotional expression, and coping strategies, we can offer empathetic and informed support to help them navigate their grief. This understanding allows us to be more sensitive and responsive when offering guidance and assistance to young people as they cope with the complexities of loss and grief in their lives.

Grief can be a challenging experience for children and adolescents, but with the right support, they can learn to cope and heal. It is important to be understanding, patient, and supportive of them during this difficult time.

Complicated Grief

Complicated grief, also known as persistent complex bereavement disorder, is a mental health condition in which an individual experiences intense and prolonged grief that significantly impacts their daily functioning and overall well-being. This form of grief goes beyond the typical grieving process and can manifest in various ways, making it difficult for the person to come to terms with the loss and move forward in their life. People experiencing complicated grief may find themselves stuck in their grieving process, unable to accept the loss or find closure. This can lead to emotional, psychological, and even physical symptoms that persist long after the loss has occurred.

This type of grief that occurs when the normal grieving process is disrupted. It is more intense and persistent than normal grief. It is often characterized by feelings of intense yearning and longing for the person who has died, as well as feelings of disbelief or anger about their death. People who experience complicated grief may also experience depression, anxiety, and physical symptoms such as insomnia or changes in appetite.

Differentiation from normal grief

While complicated grief shares some features with normal grief, it is distinguished by its prolonged nature, the intensity of the symptoms, and the significant impact on daily functioning. It is essential to differentiate between the two to provide appropriate support and intervention.

Impact on mental health

Complicated grief can have significant consequences on an individual's mental health, increasing the risk of developing depression, anxiety, substance abuse, and suicidal thoughts or behaviors. It is crucial to recognize these potential consequences and address them as part of the grieving process. Some factors that may contribute to the development of complicated grief include:

The nature of the loss

Sudden, unexpected, or particularly traumatic losses can increase the likelihood of developing complicated grief. This could include the death of a child, a violent or unexpected death, or multiple losses occurring within a short period of time.

Personal history

Individuals with a history of mental health issues, such as depression or anxiety, may be at a higher risk of experiencing complicated grief. Additionally, those with a history of unresolved past grief or trauma may be more vulnerable to developing complicated grief.

Social support

A lack of social support or understanding from friends and family can make it more challenging for someone to navigate the grieving process, potentially leading to complicated grief.

Coping mechanisms

The way an individual copes with their grief can play a role in the development of complicated grief. Maladaptive coping mechanisms, such as substance abuse or avoidance, may hinder the grieving process and contribute to the persistence of grief symptoms.

Symptoms of Complicated Grief

Here's an analysis of some common symptoms of complicated grief:

Intense and persistent longing for the deceased

While it's normal to miss a loved one after their passing,

individuals with complicated grief may experience an overwhelming and constant longing for the deceased that doesn't diminish over time.

Intrusive thoughts or images People with complicated grief may have recurring, intrusive thoughts or images related to their loved one's death, which can be distressing and interfere with daily functioning.

Difficulty accepting the loss

One key symptom of complicated grief is an inability to accept the reality of the loss, even after a significant period of time has passed.

Numbness or emotional detachment

Individuals experiencing complicated grief may feel emotionally numb or detached from others, struggling to connect with friends or family and feeling isolated in their grief.

Preoccupation with the deceased or the circumstances surrounding the death

A person with complicated grief may become excessively preoccupied with the life of the deceased, the manner of their death, or the events leading up to their passing, which can hinder their ability to focus on other aspects of life.

Intense emotional pain

Complicated grief often involves heightened emotional pain, such as feelings of anger, guilt, or sadness that persist and do not ease over time.

Disruptions in daily functioning

Complicated grief can result in significant disruptions to daily life, such as problems with work, social activities, or self-care.

Avoidance of reminders

Those experiencing complicated grief may actively avoid reminders of their loss, such as places, people, or activities associated with their loved one, due to the intense emotional pain these reminders provoke.

Loss of interest or pleasure in life

A person with complicated grief may experience a loss of interest or pleasure in activities they once enjoyed and may struggle to find meaning or purpose in their life.

Sleep disturbances

Complicated grief can lead to sleep issues, such as insomnia, nightmares, or excessive sleeping.

Physical symptoms

Individuals with complicated grief may also experience physical symptoms, such as headaches, stomachaches, or other unexplained aches and pains.

It's important to recognize that complicated grief is not a sign of weakness or a lack of resilience. Rather, it is a complex and challenging condition that may require professional support and intervention to help the individual navigate their grieving process and move toward healing.

Treatment for Complicated Grief

Treatment for complicated grief typically involves therapy, either individual or group, with a mental health professional who specializes in grief and loss. The goal of therapy is to help the person understand and process their grief, and to find ways to move forward.

Treatment involves a multifaceted approach, incorporating psychotherapy, support groups, medication, self-help strategies, and, in some cases, family therapy. By providing appropriate support, intervention, and treatment, we can help individuals navigate the complexities of complicated grief and find a path toward healing and recovery. This understanding allows us to be more sensitive and responsive when offering guidance and assistance to those who are struggling with the challenges of complicated grief in their lives.

Cognitive-Behavioral Therapy (CBT)

(CBT) is a common approach for treating complicated grief. CBT helps people identify and challenge negative thoughts and behaviors that may be contributing to their grief, and replaces them with more positive and healthy ways of thinking and coping.

Exposure therapy

This is another approach that may be used for treating complicated grief. This type of therapy involves gradually exposing the person to reminders of their loss, with the goal of helping them face and overcome their fear or avoidance of these reminders.

Psychotherapy

Various forms of psychotherapy can be beneficial for individuals experiencing complicated grief. Some evidence-based approaches include complicated grief therapy (CGT), cognitive-behavioral therapy (CBT), and interpersonal psychotherapy (IPT). These therapies can help individuals process their emotions, address unresolved aspects of the loss, and develop new coping skills.

Complicated Grief Therapy (CGT)

CGT is a specialized form of therapy designed explicitly for complicated grief. It combines elements of CBT, IPT, and exposure therapy, helping individuals confront and process their loss, develop new coping strategies, and rebuild connections with others. CGT typically involves a structured series of sessions, focusing on grief-related thoughts, emotions, and behaviors.

Support groups

Support groups can be a valuable resource for individuals experiencing complicated grief, offering a safe space to share experiences, emotions, and coping strategies with others who understand the challenges of prolonged bereavement. These groups can foster a sense of connection and empathy, helping individuals feel less isolated in their grief.

Medication

In some cases, medication may be recommended to help manage symptoms of depression, anxiety, or other mental health conditions that may be contributing to complicated grief. Antidepressants, anti-anxiety medications, or other psychotropic medications can help alleviate these symptoms and support individuals in engaging more effectively in therapy or other forms of treatment.

Self-help and self-care strategies

Encouraging individuals to practice self-help and self-care

strategies can be an essential component of treatment for complicated grief. This may involve engaging in regular exercise, maintaining a balanced diet, getting adequate sleep, practicing relaxation techniques, and staying connected with supportive friends and family.

Family therapy

In some cases, involving the family in treatment for complicated grief can be beneficial. Family therapy can help address interpersonal dynamics and communication patterns that may be contributing to the individual's complicated grief and provide support for the entire family as they navigate the grieving process together.

The role of social support

A strong social support network can be crucial for individuals experiencing complicated grief. Friends, family, and support groups can provide understanding, empathy, and encouragement, helping the individual navigate their grief and build resilience.

By providing appropriate support, intervention, and treatment, we can help individuals navigate the complexities of complicated grief and find a path toward healing and recovery. This understanding allows us to be more sensitive and responsive when offering guidance and assistance to those who are struggling with the challenges of complicated grief in their lives.

It is important to remember that everyone grieves differently and there is no one "right" way to heal. The most important thing is to find what works best for you and to seek help if needed. With time and support, it is possible to find hope and healing after loss.

Chapter 11
Moving Forward after Grief

Moving forward after the loss of a loved one can be a challenging and difficult process. However, it is important to remember that healing and recovery are possible. There are various strategies and resources available to help individuals navigate this difficult time. This is a unique and personal journey, involving the gradual process of healing and finding a new sense of meaning and purpose in life. By understanding the various aspects of moving forward after grief, we can offer appropriate support and guidance to individuals as they navigate this challenging transition.

One important aspect of moving forward after grief is to allow yourself to feel and process your emotions. It is okay to feel a range of emotions, including sadness, anger, and guilt, and it is important to give yourself time and space to work through these feelings.

Another important aspect of moving forward after grief is to engage in self-care. This can include activities such as exercise, eating well, getting enough sleep, and engaging in activities that bring you joy and relaxation.

It is also helpful to reach out to friends and family members for support and to consider seeking support from a therapist or counselor. These professionals can provide guidance and support as you navigate the grieving process and work towards finding a new sense of purpose and meaning in life. To analyze moving forward after grief, consider the following:

Acceptance and integration

One of the critical steps in moving forward after grief is accepting the reality of the loss and integrating it into one's life. This process involves acknowledging the pain and allowing oneself to experience and process the emotions associated with grief.

Rebuilding connections

As individuals move forward after grief, it is essential to rebuild connections with others and re-establish social support networks. This may involve reaching out to friends and family, joining support groups or clubs, or engaging in community activities.

Creating new routines and rituals

Establishing new routines and rituals can provide a sense of structure and continuity, helping individuals navigate their new life without their loved one. This may involve creating new traditions or modifying existing ones to honor the memory of the deceased.

Finding meaning and purpose

Moving forward after grief often involves finding new meaning and purpose in life. This may involve exploring one's values, beliefs, and passions, and pursuing activities or goals that align with these.

Embracing self-care

Prioritizing self-care is essential when moving forward after grief. This may include engaging in physical exercise, practicing relaxation techniques, maintaining a healthy diet, getting adequate sleep, and seeking professional support when needed.

Recognizing personal growth

Although grief can be a profoundly challenging experience, it can also provide opportunities for personal growth and self-discovery. Recognizing and acknowledging this growth can help individuals cultivate resilience and a deeper sense of self-awareness as they move forward.

Honoring the memory

Moving forward after grief does not mean forgetting the loved one who has passed away. Instead, it involves finding ways to honor their memory and keep their legacy alive, whether through storytelling, memorialization, or engaging in activities that were meaningful to the deceased.

Moving forward after grief is a complex and individualized process that requires acceptance, rebuilding connections, creating new routines, finding meaning and purpose, embracing self-care, recognizing personal growth, and honoring the memory of the loved one. By understanding these aspects of moving forward and offering empathetic support, we can help individuals navigate the challenges and uncertainties that come with healing from grief and finding a new sense of meaning and purpose in their lives.

Finding Meaning and Purpose After Loss

Finding meaning and purpose after loss is a complex and individual process that can help navigate the aftermath of a loss and come to terms with it. For some, finding meaning and purpose may involve honoring the memory of their loved one through volunteer work or participating in events that they know would have made their loved one proud. For others, it may involve exploring new passions or hobbies, traveling, or seeking out new experiences. Some individuals may find meaning and purpose through spirituality, religion, or other forms of faith.

Regardless of the approach, the key is to find what works for each individual and to be open to new opportunities and experiences. It's also important to be kind to oneself and recognize that there is no set timeline for finding meaning and purpose after loss. Some people may find it relatively quickly, while others may take much longer.

It can be helpful to seek support from friends, family, or a counselor to help process feelings, identify and work through any roadblocks, and explore new possibilities. Additionally, joining a support group or participating in grief-related activities can provide a sense of community and help individuals feel less alone in their journey.

Ultimately, finding meaning and purpose after loss is a process that requires patience, self-care, and an openness to new experiences and possibilities. With time and support, many individuals can find new paths forward and create a new normal after loss.

Finding meaning and purpose after experiencing a significant loss is an essential aspect of the healing process. It can help individuals make sense of their grief and build resilience as they navigate their new reality. By understanding the various ways individuals can find meaning and purpose after a loss, we can offer appropriate support and guidance during this challenging time. To find meaning and purpose after loss, consider the following:

Reflection and introspection

Encouraging individuals to reflect on their values, beliefs, and passions can help them identify new goals and directions in life. Introspection can also promote a deeper understanding of the impact of the loss and the potential for growth and transformation.

Reconnecting with spirituality or faith

For some individuals, reconnecting with their spiritual beliefs or faith can provide comfort, solace, and a sense of purpose after a loss. Engaging in prayer, meditation, or participating in religious or spiritual communities can foster a sense of connection and belonging.

Engaging in meaningful activities

Pursuing activities that align with one's values and interests can provide a sense of purpose and fulfillment. This may include volunteering, pursuing creative endeavors, engaging in advocacy work, or taking up new hobbies or interests.

Establishing new goals

Setting new personal, professional, or educational goals can help individuals find direction and motivation after a loss. These goals can provide a sense of purpose and achievement as individuals work towards them.

Fostering connections

Building and maintaining relationships with friends, family, and support networks can provide a sense of belonging and purpose. Connecting with others who have experienced similar losses can also foster a sense of understanding and empathy.

Embracing personal growth

Recognizing and embracing the personal growth that can emerge from the experience of grief can help individuals find meaning and purpose in their journey. This may involve cultivating resilience, developing empathy, or gaining a deeper understanding of oneself and one's values.

Legacy building

Honoring the memory of the deceased by engaging in activities or projects that reflect their values and passions can provide a sense of meaning and purpose. This may include creating a memorial, establishing a scholarship or charity, or participating in events or causes that were important to the loved one.

By understanding the aforementioned points and offering empathetic support, we can help individuals navigate the challenges of grief and find new meaning and purpose in their lives. This understanding allows us to be more sensitive and responsive when offering guidance and assistance to those who are struggling to find meaning and purpose after experiencing a significant loss.

Rebuilding a New Normal After Loss

Rebuilding a new normal after loss can be a difficult and challenging process, but it can also be an opportunity for growth and healing. Grief can have a profound impact on a person's life, leaving them feeling lost and unsure of how to move forward. However, with time, support, and the right tools, it is possible to rebuild a new normal and find a sense of purpose and meaning after loss.

One of the keys to rebuilding a new normal is to acknowledge and accept your feelings of grief. It is important to give yourself time to process your emotions and to recognize that grief is a journey that takes time and patience.

It is also important to reach out to friends, family, or support groups for help and comfort during this time.

In addition to seeking support, it can be helpful to engage in self-care activities that bring you comfort and joy. This can include physical activities such as exercise, practicing mindfulness and meditation, or participating in hobbies and interests that you enjoy.

Another important step in rebuilding a new normal is to find new sources of meaning and purpose in your life. This can be done by volunteering, pursuing new interests or hobbies, or focusing on your relationships with friends and family. It is important to focus on what brings you joy and fulfillment and to build a life that aligns with your values and goals.

It is also important to remember that rebuilding a new normal after loss is a gradual process, and it is okay to take things one day at a time. You may experience setbacks and challenges along the way, but with perseverance and determination, you can find a new sense of purpose and meaning after loss.

Rebuilding a new normal after experiencing a significant loss can be a challenging yet essential part of the healing process. It involves adapting to a new reality without the presence of the loved one and finding a sense of stability and balance in life. By understanding the various aspects of rebuilding a new normal, we can offer appropriate support and guidance to individuals as they navigate this transition. To build a new normal, consider the following:

Acceptance and integration

The first step in rebuilding a new normal is accepting the reality of the loss and integrating it into one's life. This process involves acknowledging the pain and allowing oneself to experience and process the emotions associated with grief.

Establishing new routines

Creating new routines and structures can provide a sense of continuity and stability, helping individuals adjust to their new reality. This may involve developing new daily habits, modifying existing traditions, or creating new rituals that honor the memory of the deceased.

Rebuilding connections

As individuals move forward, it is essential to rebuild connections with others and re-establish social support networks. This may involve reaching out to friends and family, joining support groups or clubs, or engaging in community activities.

Fostering resilience

Cultivating resilience can help individuals adapt to their new normal and overcome the challenges associated with grief. This may involve embracing self-care, seeking professional support, and recognizing the personal growth that can emerge from the experience of grief.

Nurturing emotional well-being

Prioritizing emotional well-being is crucial when rebuilding a new normal. This may include practicing self-compassion, engaging in relaxation techniques, and allowing oneself to experience a full range of emotions without judgment.

Balancing grief and daily life

Rebuilding a new normal involves finding a balance between honoring the memory of the deceased and moving forward with one's own life. This may involve setting aside dedicated time for grief while also engaging in activities that promote personal growth and well-being.

The Future After Grief

The future after grief can seem uncertain and overwhelming, but it's important to remember that it is possible to find happiness and fulfillment again. Grief is a journey and it takes time, patience, and support to work through it. It's also important to understand that everyone experiences grief differently and there is no right or wrong way to grieve.

As time goes on, people often find that they are able to start moving forward and finding meaning and purpose in their lives again. This may involve finding new passions, pursuing new interests, or seeking out new relationships. It's also important to seek support from friends, family, or mental health professionals as needed.

It's also normal for grief to resurface at various times, especially during anniversaries or special occasions. It's important to allow yourself to feel these emotions and to seek support if needed. Over time, these feelings of grief will likely become less intense and more manageable.

It's important to remember that healing from grief is a process, and it takes time and patience. It's also important to be kind to yourself and to understand that it's okay to still feel sad or overwhelmed at times. With time and support, it is possible to rebuild a new normal and to find happiness and fulfillment again after loss.

The future after grief can be uncertain and may seem daunting for those who have experienced a significant loss. However, it also holds the potential for growth, healing, and new experiences. By understanding the various aspects of the future after grief, we can offer appropriate support and guidance to individuals as they move forward and embrace the opportunities that life has to offer. To analyze the future after grief, consider the following:

Embracing healing

Healing from grief is a gradual and nonlinear process that takes time and patience. As individuals move into the future, it's essential to embrace the healing journey and allow oneself to process and integrate the emotions associated with grief.

Rediscovering joy

After a loss, it may be challenging to find joy in life again. However, embracing new experiences, engaging in activities that bring happiness, and fostering connections with loved ones can help individuals rediscover joy and cultivate a sense of well-being.

Personal growth and self-discovery

The future after grief can hold opportunities for personal growth and self-discovery. By reflecting on the loss and its impact, individuals can gain a deeper understanding of themselves, their values, and their priorities in life.

Building resilience

Cultivating resilience can help individuals adapt to the challenges of the future and navigate the uncertainties that life may bring. This may involve practicing self-care, seeking professional support, and embracing personal growth that emerges from the experience of grief.

New beginnings and opportunities

The future after grief can hold new beginnings and opportunities for individuals to explore. This may involve pursuing new interests, goals, or passions that align with their values and provide a sense of purpose and fulfillment.

Honoring the memory of the deceased

Moving into the future does not mean forgetting the loved one who has passed away. Instead, individuals can find ways to honor their memory and keep their legacy alive, whether through storytelling, memorialization, or engaging in activities that were meaningful to the deceased.

Seeking support

As individuals navigate the future after grief, it's essential to seek support from friends, family, and professional resources. This can help provide guidance, encouragement, and understanding as they move forward and embrace the opportunities that lie ahead.

Self-Care and Professional Support

Self-care involves taking care of one's physical,

emotional, and mental well-being to help manage the difficult emotions associated with loss. Self-care activities can include exercise, eating nutritious food, getting adequate sleep, and engaging in activities that bring joy and relaxation. It is also important to seek support from loved ones, friends, and professional support resources, such as a counselor or therapist if needed.

Professional support resources can provide a safe space for individuals to process their grief and work through their emotions. A trained therapist or counselor can offer coping strategies and support as the individual moves through their grief journey. Additionally, support groups can provide a sense of community and a space to connect with others who are also grieving.

Self-care and professional support are essential components of navigating the grieving process and rebuilding one's life after a significant loss. These resources can help individuals maintain their emotional and physical well-being while providing guidance, understanding, and coping strategies throughout their healing journey. To enhance self-care and professional support, consider the following:

Prioritizing self-care

Practicing self-care involves nurturing one's physical, emotional, and mental well-being. This may include engaging in activities that promote relaxation, maintaining a healthy lifestyle, and setting aside dedicated time for rest and self-reflection.

Seeking professional support

Professional support, such as therapy or counseling, can provide individuals with a safe space to process their emotions and gain insights into their grief. Trained professionals can offer guidance, coping strategies, and resources tailored to the unique needs of the individual.

Joining support groups

Support groups offer a sense of community and understanding, allowing individuals to connect with others who have experienced similar losses. These groups can provide emotional support, practical advice, and a sense of belonging during the grieving process.

Fostering connections

Building and maintaining relationships with friends, family, and support networks can help provide a sense of belonging and emotional support during difficult times. Reaching out to loved ones and sharing one's experiences can foster understanding and empathy.

Setting boundaries

Setting boundaries and communicating one's needs to others can help protect one's emotional well-being and ensure that adequate time and space are dedicated to the grieving process.

Embracing mindfulness and relaxation techniques

Practicing mindfulness and relaxation techniques, such as meditation, deep breathing, or yoga, can help manage stress and promote emotional well-being during the grieving process.

Acknowledging and validating emotions

Allowing oneself to experience and validate the full range of emotions associated with grief is an essential aspect of self-care. This may involve journaling, expressing emotions through art or music, or simply acknowledging one's feelings without judgment.

By understanding these aforementioned and offering empathetic support, we can help individuals navigate the uncertainties and challenges of the future while embracing the potential for growth, healing, and new experiences. This understanding allows us to be more sensitive and responsive when offering guidance and assistance to those who are moving forward after experiencing a significant loss, helping them face the future with hope and resilience.

www.ingramcontent.com/pod-product-compliance
Lightning Source LLC
Chambersburg PA
CBHW060040150626
46553CB00017BA/603